Country Roads
~ of ~
MINNESOTA

A Guide Book
from Country Roads Press

Country Roads
~ of ~
MINNESOTA

Martin Hintz

Illustrated by Cliff Winner
Cover Illustration by Victoria Sheridan

Country Roads Press

C A S T I N E • M A I N E

Country Roads of Minnesota
© 1994 by Martin Hintz. All rights reserved.

Published by Country Roads Press
P.O. Box 286, Lower Main Street
Castine, Maine 04421

Text and cover design by Edith Allard.
Cover illustration by Victoria Sheridan.
Illustrations by Cliff Winner.
Typesetting by Camden Type 'n Graphics.

ISBN 1–56626–027–8

Library of Congress Cataloging-in-Publication Data
Hintz, Martin.
    Country roads of Minnesota / Martin Hintz.
        p.   cm.
    Includes index.
    ISBN 1-56626-027-8 : $9.95
    1. Minnesota—Tours.   2. Automobile travel—
Minnesota—Guidebooks.   I. Title.
F604.3.H56   1994
917.7604'53—dc20   94-14331
                                                                CIP

Printed in the United States of America.
10 9 8 7 6 5 4 3 2 1

To my mother, Gertrude Hintz,
who first showed me the way.

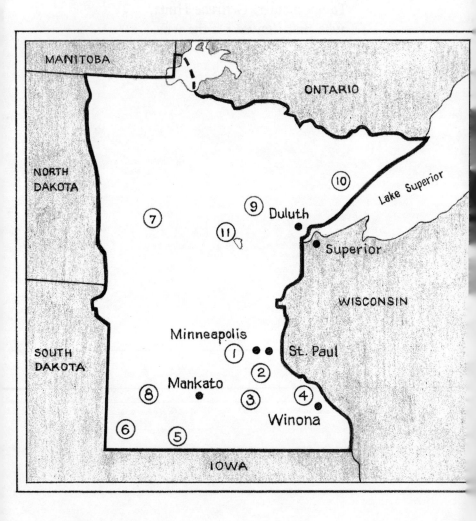

Contents

(& Key to Minnesota Country Roads)

Acknowledgments

Special thanks should be extended to the staff of the Minnesota Division of Tourism, especially Tom Craig's, and to Paul Huguenot and his coworkers at the Minnesota Department of Agriculture. And thanks to everyone from Faribault to Fairmont and Wayzata to Worthington who offered suggestions for the manuscript, proudly showed off their favorite country roads, shared their apple cider and homemade wine, opened museum doors, pointed the way to vistas and valleys, demonstrated how to catch walleye, and generally were there when needed. After all, that's the Minnesota spirit. I now have a greater appreciation for wild and cultivated rice, for Minnesota apples, for the state's piemakers, the colors of autumn, the freshness of the air, and the ways of the Native Americans who were here first.

Readers of *Country Roads of Minnesota may also* enjoy the *Minnesota Travel Companion: A Unique Guide to the History Along Minnesota's Highways* by Richard Olsenius (Bluestem Productions, Wayzata, 1982, $14.95). Vintage photos accompany his historical roadway vignettes.

Introduction

Minnesota—the land of lakes, of muskies, of art works, of ballet, of Paul Bunyan and blue oxen the size of warehouses. A mix of the wild and the urban, with thousands of open square miles and more Hmong restaurants than almost any other state in the nation. Minnesota is a classy yet neighborly place that loves equally well handpainted silk and red flannel, where cross-country skis line garage walls next to Mercedes autos. It's a shame that the state is a secret to anyone east of the Appalachians and west of the Rockies.

Moose and bear, darn right. But it's also home to internationally recognized art centers and tough golf courses.

The land rolls out a carpet of pines, oaks, and birches. Dotted with thousands of brilliantly sparkling lakes, the state twinkles and winks when seen via a passing airplane. A city or village then pops out of the mosaic, waving its obvious hello to the wanderer.

Since I was a kid, I've regularly visited Minnesota. First, there were the summertime trips to relatives in Minneapolis, then a stint at St. Paul's University of St. Thomas, and now trips to see my sister and her family in Bloomington, on Minneapolis' far south fringe. It was always a state for exploration, especially driving north from Iowa, where I grew up only a forty-five-minute ride from the Minnesota border. I now live in Wisconsin, where it's still an easy run to the Mississippi River and a swift crossing to the Land of Sky Blue Waters (thanks, Hamms!).

Often writing about the state for numerous publications, I found that not everyone there is a Norwegian (although it's a close call). There is an ethnic mix that ranges from Dakota Sioux to Latvians, from Chinese to Hispanics. This potpourri of people provides a stellar lineup of festivals, eateries, and customs that augment the grand Midwest tradition of down-home American. There are a multitude of back roads and country escapes even near the glittering Twin Cities, a megalopolis combo of trendy Minneapolis and careful St. Paul. Each area of the state has its distinct personality, best explored in person, to be savored and then talked about. Hiking and driving fit hand-in-glove when it comes to Minnesota. It's one thing to drive "there" and another to park and walk the streets and the trails to discover the richness of Minnesota life.

Often liberal to the point of left (so what!), with a heritage of concern for its residents in the Hubert H. Humphrey stump-pounding, get-things-done mode, Minnesota is also the home of marvelous personalities and amazing places. Little Falls was the boyhood stomping ground of Charles (Lucky Lindy, the Lone Eagle) Lindbergh, who flew the Atlantic single-handedly. The Hull-Rust-Mahoning Mine near Hibbing is the largest open-pit mine in the world (covering 1,275 acres).

Folks are rightly proud of living in the state with the northernmost pinpoint of the continental United States. The Northwest Angle State Forest and the Red Lake Indian Reservation are actually more north than Maine's tip-top, taking a healthy nibble out of the bottom of Canada's Ontario. Take that, you folks out East!

When we were kids, my cousin Edna and her husband Art would take my sister and me to fishing retreats with by now long-forgotten names, after what seemed lengthy drives out from the urban nort' side of Minneapolis where they lived. Raised as we were among the cornfields of Iowa, seeing all those towering pines was amazing. Still is. And fish! Lunkers bigger than The Ark itself, at least to seven-year-old eyes used to grumpy bullheads found along our murky Wap-sipinicon far to the south.

These days, there are even more enjoyable activities: watching Stillwater's Civil War muster in October, participating in the John Beargrease Sled Dog Marathon near Duluth in January, hiking the Angleworm Trail in the Superior National Forest, Oz-ing through June's Judy Garland festival in Grand Rapids, observing bald eagles at the Reads Landing observatory, waving to bashful Amish kids near Harmony, reveling in the lazy wonderfulness of bed and breakfast retreats from Winona to who knows where.

Minnesota, here we come again. Older, wiser, and ready for action.

For all the tips and help you can absorb, contact the Minnesota Office of Tourism, 100 Metro Square, 121 7th Place East, St. Paul, MN 55101-2112. 800-657-3700.

Directories of campgrounds, resorts, and accommodations are available, covering even the most remote sections of the state for the hard-core Country Roads explorer. The state also has all-inclusive fliers on biking, canoeing, skiing and snowmobiling. The info folks will also answer specific questions.

The state has several excellent free directories that outline "minitours" in southern, northeastern, and north central/western Minnesota. Within the publications are maps, attractions, phone numbers and addresses, area highlights, and plenty of photos to pump up the travel adrenalin.

For details on state parks, forests, and trails, the Minnesota Department of Natural Resources is a valuable resource in its own right. Contact the agency at 500 Lafayette Rd., Box 40, St. Paul, MN 55155. 612-296-6157, or 800-766-6000 inside Minnesota.

Don't forget to call any local chamber of commerce or small-town convention and visitors bureau for the latest on what's happening on Main Street or in the countryside.

Maps and other travel planning guides are available from any of the twelve state Highway Information Centers located at twelve major entry points into Minnesota. Restroom facilities, dog-walking areas, and brochure racks are available there, as well. For general travel information, call 800-657-3700 (in Canada, call 800-766-8687).

The best part of Country Roads exploration is reaching out to people. Minnesotans, whether sunburned prairie farmers or forestland hunters, talk with guests. Simply say "hello" and be prepared to chat. Minnesotans generally want to know about you and what brought you to their state, as well. They are justifiably proud of what they can offer on the fun front—subzero winters and all. So what if the truck-size mosquito is the state bird. Minnesota loons are even nicer.

Now to the basic question: Lake Wobegon, are you there?

To find out, the *Minnesota Atlas & Gazetteer* could provide an answer. This is one of the best topographical map books available, with its seventy-seven easy-to-read quadrangular maps that show enough trails and highways to satisfy the most inveterate Country Roads explorer. For a copy, contact the DeLorme Mapping Company, Box 298, Freeport, ME 04032. 207-865-4171. The company says that a reader wishing to create a wall mosaic of Minnesota needs to join all the maps from two of the atlases to prevent misalignment. The result will be a hanging 10 feet wide by 11.5 feet high. With a view like that, one can almost spot the moose moving through the sloughs around Pot Hole Lake in the Boundary Waters Canoe Wilderness Area.

Good luck and happy Country Roads driving.

Background

Before hitting the Country Roads of Minnesota, a traveler
needs to know some of the basics: the who, what, where,
why, when, and how. Longer than wider (406 miles from
north to south and about 200 miles from east to west at its
skinniest point mid-state), Minnesota is bordered on the
north by Canada, the south by Iowa, the east by Wisconsin,
and the west by the Dakotas. The state can be divided into
three distinct terrains: the grassy prairies in the west, the pine
forests of the north, and the hardwood forests of the east.

Only about 10,000 years ago, the landscape was covered
by glaciers. When they melted, lakes and rivers were created,
making more shoreline than California, Florida, and Hawaii
combined. While the state license plate says "Land of 10,000
Lakes," there are actually at least 12,000 that have been
mapped. Coming up with names has been a challenge for
surveyors. There are only so many Big Lake, Little Lake, Fish
Lake, and Lake Lake appellations to go around. In fact, there
are 201 Mud and 154 Long lakes. So name-callers started into
One-Mile Lake, Two-Mile Lake, and so on. And there is even
a Swan Lake (in Nicollet County, six miles east of New Ulm).
Some of the best names are Bologna, Diddle de Woddle, and
Dismal Swamp lakes. There are 11,842 lakes of more than ten
acres, with one boat for every six people.

The state received its name from the Dakota Sioux, who
called their country *"Minisota,"* which means "sky-tinted
waters."

In keeping with the state's water theme, the Mississippi River, which rises at Lake Itasca, is the third longest river in the world at 2,552 miles. The Minnesota Office of Tourism points out that Minnesota's water flows in three directions: north to Canada's Hudson Bay, east to the Atlantic Ocean, and south to the Gulf of Mexico. No water flows into the state.

Here are some quiz items to keep the kids busy while driving the Country Roads:

- State bird: common loon
- State tree: Norway pine
- State gemstone: Lake Superior agate
- State fish: walleye pike
- State flower: pink and white Yellow Lady Slipper
- State mushroom: morel
- State muffin: blueberry
- State drink: milk

When Minnesotans aren't fishing, which 2.3 million state residents are recording doing every year (half the state population), they are farming, logging, mining, and working in tourism—if not in a bank, insurance company, library, or butcher shop.

Armed with these important details, you can now hit the road.

1 ~

Excelsior-Wayzata

Getting there: From Minneapolis take I-394/US 12 to State 101 to Wayzata Boulevard and Wayzata; or I-394 to I-494 to State 7 to Excelsior.

Highlights: *Lake Minnetonka restaurants and parks; Wayzata Depot; Old Log Theater; art galleries; bookstores; University of Minnesota Landscape Arboretum; Lake Minnetonka Antique and Classic Boat Rendezvous; clothing and specialty gift shops.*

There are remote, fog-shrouded country roads less traveled. But there are others where meandering can still be fun even though contemporary life has installed curbs where prairie grasses once touched the horizon.

Whenever the urban rush became too much, Twin Citians once retreated to Lake Minnetonka, just a whisper west of Minneapolis. Today it takes about thirty minutes from downtown by bus or suburban minivan or twenty minutes by roaring sports car (some drivers say twelve minutes) to reach the neighborhood that was once THE country resort. For generations, Big City's bankers, brewers, bakers, and burghers

1

packed up kids, picnic baskets, and blankets for a run to the lake district and its fabled beaches. In those days, these jaunts were truly expeditions, rivaling any safaris to the nether regions. Laden with baloney sandwiches, beer bottles, and sun umbrellas, families journeyed by train or trolley to what was the edge of the known world. Some of the luckier wealthy eventually built huge estates on this frontier, capturing soft summer breezes from porches the size of ballrooms.

All has not been turned-to-town, however. The Baker Park Reserve along US 12 and County 19 near Lake Independence still offers camping, with swimming, hiking, fishing, a playground, and picnic areas. The campgrounds are about a twenty-minute drive north of what is called the "West Upper Lake" of Lake Minnetonka, with US 12 carrying tourists to Wayzata, one of the major resort towns on the lake.

In the mind's eye of a contemplative traveler, the main lake remains, well, almost the same. The graveled trails are now paved. Many of the mansions' rolling lawns have been chopped up into a more or less tasteful suburban maze. Bayberry shrubs and Scotch pine windbreaks delineate lots. Yet, a day drive around the lake is still a restful getaway, because open spaces and paths leading to the lake remain. On an early summer's jaunt, hopscotching from highway to side road to back lane, you can revel in the fresh scent of green: from newly mown lawns to old, old money.

As the knowledgeable say in the Twin Cities, all roads lead to the Lake Country. Take I-35W north or south to what the locals call the I-694/494 "Great Circle" route. Drive west to the I-494/State 7 intersection for a southerly jaunt beginning in Excelsior, or take the I-494/US 12 off-ramp to Wayzata for starting along the north shore. The Metropolitan Transit System buses service the area, as well.

This is a land still in touch with itself, despite trendy road names like Lake Lucy or Lynwood. Even the gated subdivisions with their upscale flora and fauna titles can't diminish the beauty.

Long a sacred reserve for the Sioux, the lake was the spiritual home of Manitou, the Great Spirit. Keeping a watch over the rolling blue-green waters was the spirit Me-ne-a-ton-ka, after whom the lake received its name. The lake is about twenty-seven miles long, but its shoreline is estimated to be some 110 miles due to convoluted inlets hacksawed out of the earth by Ma Nature.

Enchanted Island, its name evoking a Peter Pan landing strip, is now the village of Shorewood. The island, the traditional site of many Native American ceremonies, is reached by the Zimmerman Pass bridge from Tuxedo Boulevard.

The Minnetonka area had been known to whites as early as 1822. In that year, a drummer boy from the newly built Fort Snelling fifteen miles to the east stumbled upon the lake. He wound up at Gray's Bay, the lake's most easterly touch, and met a band of friendly Chippewa. The young soldier was the last official white visitor for the next several decades. The tribe was left in peace for the next thirty years, until Minnesota Governor Ramsey visited the lake and made the name "Minnetonka" the official tag. Next to show up was the Excelsior Pioneer Association, a contingent of land-hungry settlers from New York state who whacked their way through the pines into the neighborhood.

The band of hale and hearty entrepreneurs was lured to Minnesota by tales of woodland riches espoused by smooth-talking developer George Bertram. The association founded the village of Excelsior in 1853, building homes and establishing schools. Within five years, the original Chippewa had departed, probably because of all that hammering and sawing.

(As a historical sidelight, a number of intrepid descendants of those first Yankee opportunists left Excelsior for

Alaska, to stake out claims in the gold stampede of the 1890s. Adventure was in their genes.)

Rail service was established from Minneapolis to Excelsior in 1882, bringing tourists to revel in what was considered the countryside's healthier climes. Bravely, the pink-cheeked vacationers faced down Minnesota's legendary mosquito population, at first camping out before resorts, amusement parks, and gift shops were built. When the construction boom came, the glittering Lake Park Hotel, the Sampson House, the Excelsior House, and the White House were considered the ultimate in luxury by their wide-eyed urban guests. Steamers, such as the *Belle of Minnetonka* and the *City of St. Louis*, huffed and puffed over the lake during these golden years, transporting thousands of vacationers on their summer getaways.

In Wayzata, however, St. Paul rail magnate James J. Hill was peeved when locals refused to grant his first choice of right-of-way into their new village. He had planned on laying his St. Paul and Pacific railroad line along the community's main street, thereby blocking Wayzata's access to Minneapolis. The town sued Hill and suggested that he move the railroad to a neighboring street. Hill, nicknamed the Empire Builder, was not the kind of magnate who would take recommendations from anyone.

So he shifted the tracks one mile out of town and swore that the audacious Wayzatians would have to "walk a mile for the next twenty years" to hitch a ride on his trains. However, as he aged, Hill eventually moved the railroad back into town in 1906, constructing the depot that currently doubles as the Greater Wayzata Area Chamber of Commerce. A parade and an arts and crafts fair highlight James J. Hill Days each September, demonstrating that locals have long forgotten that old feud. Throughout the summer, the depot is the focal point for free concerts. In February, when winter's raw wind whistles in from the lake, hearty folks cluster around the depot to revel in the Chilly Open, which features twenty-seven holes of golf on frozen Lake Minnetonka. A pancake breakfast and reaaaal-llly hot chili make the weather tolerable.

Yet, as the town expanded, Hill's rail line effectively cut everyone off from the Lake Minnetonka beach, resulting in generations of kids who learned how important it was to look both ways before dashing over to the water. Curmudgeon Hill's last locomotive roared through town in 1971, but the roadbed was left in place. Wayzata's "lower" downtown, what is now a long strip of upscale clothing, souvenir, sand-wich, and furniture shops, still fronts the rail line. The "uptown," with its banks, strip malls, and parking lots, is further back from the lake and safely removed from where the trains used to rumble.

The best place to stop on a Wayzata Sunday summer morn is at the cathedral-like Minnetonka Boat Works. Once inside, take a look at the silk-screened sailing sweatshirts and blinding day-glo rafting tubes on your way to morning buns and juice. Ogle, if you will, the $270,000 forty-three-foot Por-tofino power yacht rocking quayside as it awaits a buyer. The boat appears the size of a battleship when seen close at hand. Once you are past these temptations with wallet intact, the view of the lake sets the mind and heart at ease.

"Oh, yes," affirm salesmen Geoff Mautz and Dan Gau, the Boat Works sells about seven or so of the Portofinos yearly. Purchasers are usually dual-home Twin Citians who escape Minnesota's frosty winter breath by condo-ing on the Gulf Coast. There's also a good drop-in trade from itinerant businessfolk who reside in Australia and the Far East. It seems that they buy yachts after a morning of munching at Sasha's, leaving with full stomachs and plenty of pocket change. Eleven mechanics are on duty to accommodate such really serious boaters who want the oil checked before ship-ment overseas.

For the ordinary person interested in simple family fish-ing, the Boat Works also has an assortment of the standard

Cajun 174ZWs, with price tags of $15,900. Of course, each comes with a 115-horsepower Yamaha engine and custom Trailboss trailer that includes a boarding ladder and in-water delivery. Don't forget to ask about the two glassed-in translucers on the speedy-o craft. Cane pole is not included.

Past the depot, about two blocks up Lake Street, is Woullet's Bakery, which whips up what discerning munchers consider Cookies-to-Die-For. The English toffee, sugar, and Swedish raisin are the best. But each display case bursts with sweet-tooth temptations, so load up. A dozen cookies are only $3. Woullet's apple raisin coffee cake should be banned for being destructive to dieters, yet purchase one anyway for the next leg of a back-country/kind-of-city drive. One never knows what rigors might be encountered down the block and around the corner. Eating everything on the spot could mean spending the rest of the day walking Wayzata to work off calories. Or simply take a bag of cookies aboard the free Wayzata Trolley. From the historic train depot, it takes visitors along Lake Street, on to the edge of town, and back again to the beach.

Leaving town via Wayzata Boulevard, link up with State 101 to traverse the eastern end of the lake. The roadway rolls between Wayzata and Gray's bays, looping through the villages of Woodland, Deephaven, and Greenwood. The latter is home of the 655-seat Old Log Theater, one of the oldest continuously running community theaters in the country, having been founded on May 31, 1940. Open fifty-two weeks a year, the resident Equity company performs two shows a year. A wearer of many hats, Don Stolz is currently producer/director/owner. Stolz took over the theater in 1946 after being an actor and director there in 1941 and 1942. To find the nine-and-a-half-acre site tucked into its groves of firs and maples, follow the signs along State 7. Comedy productions such as *Don't Dress for Dinner* by French writer Martin Campoletti and *Run for Your Wife* attract motor coach tours fresh from shoppping sprees at nearby Bloomington's expansive Mall of America. The original theater has been converted into a workshop, but the rough-sawed cedar main building preserves the ambience of the first structure.

On the way to Excelsior are numerous antique shops for dangerous browsing and buying. The Corner Door, Crafters Mall, Carrousel Antiques of Wayzata, Carrol Shepherd's Consignment shop, and Deephaven Antiques and Jewelry are a few of the stores where the look of great-grandma's era has a contemporary polish and pizzazz.

For the sports-minded, there's good bicycling along McGinty, Ridgewood, and Vine Hill roads and the abandoned Minneapolis-St. Paul rail bed through these residential districts. Or pedal along Minnetonka Boulevard, cutting over the shallow waters of Carson's Bay and down toward St. Alban's and Excelsior bays. Once in Excelsior, pick the bike trail behind the Excelsior Mill shopping complex, formerly an old lumberyard on Water Street.

Although this area can no longer claim to be a country space, a visitor can still capture a sense of Mother Earth by exiting the main thoroughfares. For instance, leave State 7 on Christmas Lake Road. The short back run parallels the highway, taking motorists to the Oak Hill cemetery. From a bluff, this settler burial ground overlooks the sprawling backside of the new South Lake Minnetonka Public Safety Office.

The cemetery's narrow, dirt lane entrance cuts into the left side of the ridge just off Christmas Lake, taking a careful driver to the top for a stroll amid tilted tombstones. There's an adrenalin rush on the return drive down, as you hope the car won't tumble onto the softball fields near the cop shop. Folks here take their ballgames seriously. An upended car at third base would present a distinct impediment on the way to home plate.

The Bates family sleeps near the cemetery's oak-shaded peak, buried in plots near the McCormick, Delfrie, and Haralson clans—the names demonstrating Minnesota's ethnic montage. In the 1920s, local-boy-who-made-good Charles Haralson developed a winter-keeping apple that has become one of the state's most famous fruit crops (an earlier Excelsior resident, Peter Gideon, worked for forty years to perfect the luscious Wealthy apple).

After a safe descent out of the cemetery, stop to say howdy to Patrolman Allan Fink. As a native who used to deliver *Minneapolis Star-Tribune* newspapers around the region, Fink talks readily about growing up in what has become a patchwork of bedroom communities. Soft-spoken Fink admits it helps to know the favorite teenage necking hangouts—a needed detail at 11:00 P.M. curfew time, especially after a Minnetonka High School Skippers football game. Excelsior hasn't had its own high school since 1951, and all the kids now attend the community-wide school.

"We welcome visitors, not speeders," Fink asserts in part-welcome, part-warning tones. "But if you're in trouble, don't hesitate to call 911."

A must-stop in Excelsior is the Christopher Inn, a rambling white bed and breakfast with a porch that just won't quit. The inn, built as a summer home for Minneapolis's Wyer family at the turn of the century, is on the National Register of Historic Places. Like a gingerbread palace, the house sits on a rise at 201 Mill Street overlooking the Five Corners intersection (Excelsior Boulevard and Mill, Lake, Morse, and 2nd streets).

A giggle of youngsters plays an old-fashioned round of croquet on the side lawn, while mom and innkeeper Joan Johnson takes a mid-morning break from bedmaking. A slim, energetic woman, she and her husband Howard ("No Howard Johnson jokes, please," she pleads) have run the bed and breakfast since 1985. The inn is homey, where kids are definitely welcome, but (warning!) reservations are not accepted from unmarried couples. Working fireplaces, intricate woodwork, and spacious rooms make the Christopher Inn a popular site as a backdrop for wedding photographs.

The original owners had seven children, which made the house a real find for the Johnsons, who had been looking for a distinguished property with plenty of bedrooms. There was a generational kinship, as well, since the Johnsons also have seven youngsters (David, Christopher, Paul, Ann, Peter, Mary, and Mark). Guests, however, won't tumble over dolls, frisbees, or toddlers' togs on the sweeping front staircase, because the hotelier family currently lives in a home behind the Big House.

As it has for more than a century, Excelsior still caters to the tourist crowd, with its potpourri of gift shops and T-shirt outlets. Park anywhere along Lake Street and walk to C.C. Graham's Frog Island Book Shop, one of the best independent bookstores in southeastern Minnesota. Frog Island has been a main street staple for a generation of Excelsiorites. In addition to a delightfully extensive selection of children's books by the likes of Sherry Garland, the shop also offers shelves of local histories. Clerk Ben Sousa can easily pull up a winner, perfect for late night snuggling and a cup of tea at the Christopher Inn.

One of the best works for background on Lake Minnetonka architecture is the *Historic Site Book*, published in 1984 by the Excelsior Preservation Commission. There is still a Frog Island, a rocky promontory about 200 feet offshore, but adventurous kids don't play there anymore as they used to before the Television Era, laments Nina Stark, a longtime resident who doubles as executive secretary of the Excelsior Chamber of Commerce. Her husband, Paul, a former mayor of Excelsior, has been recently elected to the city council. He ran for this office because he wanted to remain in touch with the changing times. "Keeps him active," she confides.

Stark's two-story cedar-shake home, built in 1938, doubles as the chamber office. Her tidy lawn runs down to blue-green College Lake, packed with a flotilla of gabbling wood ducks and honking Canada geese. The lake used to be the town skating rink, where ice palaces were built in the winter and youthful romances kept the winter wind at bay.

Excelsior Amusement Park was an entertainment staple for the Twin Cities from 1924 to 1974, when rising costs forced its shuttering. Excelsior Park Tavern, near Oak Hill Cemetery, now occupies the site. The tavern, actually a no-need-to-wear-neckties restaurant, still offers thrilling kiddie rides salvaged from the old park.

Although it's not quite the same as when seventy-year-old Oscar Babcock used to loop-the-loop there in the 1930s, the Excelsior Park Tavern still rates as a worthy eatery when you're driving through Minnetonka country. On his bike, the dapper Babcock would roar down a 100-foot incline, flip upside down, and then leap a forty-foot gap, to hit the ground pedaling frantically. His nightly thrill show (twice on Sundays) was a favorite draw during the Depression. Everyone was disappointed if Babcock's run (for the princely weekly sum of $400) was put off because of wind and rain. Babcock, of course, was no dummy.

Local author and historian Bob Williams wrote two historical novels centering on the area: *Excelsior* and *Good Luck on Your Downward Journey*. In 1934, people didn't have much money so they'd come out to the amusement park to watch daredevils plunge into water. Just before a diver would climb out onto the tottering platform for the leap into space, the announcer would holler, "Get ready. And good luck on your downward journey." These days, courageous local sports (fortified at the tavern) can bungee jump throughout the summer, leaping from a tower erected for the purpose.

At the corner of Lake and Water streets, at the foot of downtown Excelsior, bob the *Queen of Excelsior, Paradise Char-*

ters, and *Lady of the Lake* charter excursion boats. Across the street is Haskell's roomy Port of Excelsior pub/restaurant, catering to the docksider set since 1934. The informal eatery offers a $2.99 lunch from 11:00 A.M. to 2:30 P.M. Eat in or take out, the signs say. Call 474-0937 for hauling away.

Haskell's is a hangout for the community's softball and rugby teams, which get a free pitcher of beer if they show up in uniform (if other guests can down two pitchers, they get the third one free). Barkeep Tom Clark and his waitress staff are kept busy filling orders each evening when a sports contingent bursts in.

Outside the Port of Excelsior, Lynn Cowles stops to chat. As a former member of the planning commission, Cowles is one of the city's biggest boosters. She assures passing writers that the town is full of interesting individualists, but even after fourteen years living there, the old-timers still consider her a newcomer. "Actually," she confides, "it's unusual to be born in Excelsior anyway. There isn't a local hospital here."

This lack of on-site birthing services has never been much of a problem in Excelsior. The beloved Dr. Hugh Arey, who died in 1934, delivered most of the folks over age sixty who live in town. Arey was typical of the rural medical practitioner who was often bedside from births to deaths for his patients. At the Water Street and State 19 junction, a memorial obelisk in his honor is surrounded by a brilliant display of flaming roses, crimson geraniums, and golden marigolds. Benches are put there in the summer where strollers can pause for a rest and contemplation. Across Water Street, the high school, built in 1929, is being remodeled and recycled into an elementary school. It will service the burgeoning numbers of kids from throughout the area.

Excelsior is a town in touch with its past.

Since 1922, Mason Chrysler-Plymouth has been a staple of downtown Excelsior. The dealership was started by the father and uncle of current owner Bill Mason. Frank and Ray

Mason had originally dealt in the long-forgotten Moon and Star autos. In 1926, they cast their lot with Chrysler-Plymouth, which seemed a more up-and-coming auto firm. The cars are certainly less expensive than the yachts at the Boat Works across the lake.

Olds Dry Goods, built as an Odd Fellows Hall in 1897, has been in the same family since 1929. Jim Olds, the smiling grandson of the first owner, still runs the comfortably crowded shop, offering a potpourri of products from postcards to geegaws. On bustling 3rd Street, just across from the old grade school, the crumbling Food Growers Building stands, but just barely. Before refrigeration, vegetables and fruit would be stored in the dark, cool basement there, prior to being shipped by train to the nearby cities. The oaken floorboards were separated to allow circulation. Old-timers in Excelsior tell of the wonderful perfume of fresh strawberries in their dampened wooden baskets.

After leaving Excelsior on State 7, travel west to Edge Boulevard (County 44) for a run up the western side of the lake. The road bridges Halsted Bay before running into Shoreline Drive (State 15) and a jaunt along the northern beaches and back into Wayzata. On the way is Mound, where the world-famous Tonka Toys had been made for generations of tiny construction equipment fans. The plant was shuttered in the mid-1980s when manufacture of the rugged little trucks was moved to Juarez, Mexico.

Park at any of the many boat launches along State 15, roll down the car windows, and tune into the sounds of summer: the tinkle of mast chains on moored sailboats, the rumble of motorboats, the shouts and splashing of sunburned kids leaping from the end of a dock.

In the vicinity of Spring Park Bay, barely visible from the highway concrete near the Black Lake Bridge, hides a small wooden pier. Partially submerged and delightfully tilted for

Satisfy your chub-fishing fever in Lake Mennetonka

an extra touch of pretend danger, the sagging platform is perfect for a freckled ten-year-old in a wide straw hat. With his cane pole and dangling line, he's satisfying his chub-fishing fever in the cool waters of Lake Minnetonka. Cicadas chirrup in the yellowing ragweed, and a cloud-white gull hacks overhead in the faraway sharp blue sky. Grumbling traffic noises fade and, for one kid's twentieth-century afternoon, it's Country Roads time again.

In the Area

Wayzata Chamber of Commerce (Wayzata): 612-473-9595

Minnetonka Boat Works (Wayzata): 612-473-7305

Woullet Bakery (Wayzata): 612-473-8621

Old Log Theater (Greenwood): 612-474-5951

Excelsior Chamber of Commerce (Excelsior): 612-474-6461

Christopher Inn (Excelsior): 612-474-6816

Frog Island Book Store (Excelsior): 612-474-7612

Minnesota Renaissance Festival (Shakopee): 612-445-7361

Minnesota Zoo (Apple Valley): 612-432-9000

University of Minnesota Landscape Arboretum
    (Chanhassen): 612-443-2460

Valley Fair Amusement Park (Shakopee): 612-445-7600

2 ~

Northfield-Hastings

Getting there: From the Twin Cities, take I-35W south and turn east on State 19 to Northfield. Pick up the Old Wheat Road (Dakota County 47) to Hastings. Return to Minneapolis-St. Paul via US 61/10 or any number of other roads (52, 55, 56, 71 or 95).

Highlights: *Farm communities, historical town museums, Defeat of Jesse James festival, popcorn wagons, bed and breakfasts, and loads of wheat.*

Oz-like, the Twin Cities recede in the rearview mirror as you cruise down I-35W. Glittering towers of glass and steel shimmer magically on the central Minnesota prairie, captured by the morning's ballet-dancing light. Designed by Japanese, Finns, and homegrown architectural talent, the Cities' buildings are slippered with a fringe of forest. From this distance, with the new sun reflecting from thousands of windows, Minneapolis and St. Paul are blazing candles.

Once you have left Bloomington, home of the vast 500-store Mall of America, the Minnesota River Valley is a major geographical highpoint. The five-mile-wide, 250-foot rift in the earth was gouged out by a retreating glacial backwater 12,000 years ago. In those days, that body of water was called Lake Agassiz, larger than the combined Great Lakes.

Swooping along I-35W, you might expect to see a pig-tailed and pinafored girl with her tiny dog merrily leading a tin woodsman, a lion, and a scarecrow back to the gleaming castle-like Foshay Tower and any resident wizard there. But as the freeway rollercoasters on to the south toward Albert Lea, the Emerald City eventually disappears and the road remains clear of storybook characters.

The highway slides into Dakota County, named after a federation of seven Native American tribes that once roamed Minnesota. Called Nadoussioux or "enemy" by the Chippewa, the Dakota became commonly known as Sioux. Their villages once dotted this area. The principal sites were Kaposia, today's South St. Paul; Medicine Bottle's encampment at Pine Bend on the Mississippi; and Black Dog's tepees at a bend of the Minnesota River where contemporary Burnsville is located.

Dakota County's hills were pushed up by the last of the giant ice sheets that rumbled out of Canada and into the Red and Minnesota river valleys. That ice ledge, several thousand feet in places, extended all the way into Iowa. When the ice eventually melted, it fathered the Vermillion and Cannon rivers.

Turning east off the interstate onto State 19, you have only about a thirty-minute drive to Northfield for another country road adventure, even without the Dakotas, Chippewa, or Dorothy and her fantasy friends. The drive is peaceful and uneventful, except for glimpses of soaring red-tailed hawks.

It's a relief to get away from the concrete slash of freeway and into the countryside, where prosperous farms dapple the land. The buildings are speckles of color amid the fields of waving brown wheat and still-green corn. White or red barns, shiny metallic pole sheds, and squat henhouses cluster around the feet of the A. O. Smith Harvestore blue silos. Piercing the cloudless sky, with painted American flags frozen to their vastly fat, curved surfaces, the silos are frontier watchtowers ringing the faraway city.

State 19 is quiet, with only a few grunting, downshifting eighteen-wheelers, floating as battleships along the two-lane. It's an easy cruise east into the Home of Malt-O-Meal, thirty miles south of the Twin Cities. But first, there's the inclined driveway to the left, leading to the lush lawns of St. Olaf College. Its graduates include two Minnesota governors and Barry Morrow, Oscar- and Emmy-winning author who wrote the screenplays for *Bill* and *The Rain Man*, among others. The city's other highly respected university, Carlton College, is on the other side of town, also on State 19.

Then a roadside sign greets motorists: "Northfield, A Special Space." Just beyond it, you can pull into the parking lot at the M-O-M plant. In the lobby, receptionist Del Rose says a friendly hello. Her T-shirt, on this day-off Saturday, reads "Love Snickers," attesting to her love of that candy bar. The site is where Jesse Ames built a mill in the mid-1800s to render the area's wheat into flour. Ames's flour won a prize at the 1876 Philadelphia Exposition. Donavon Pautzke, retired vice president, is busy working on the company history these days, with promises that a pamphlet will be ready shortly.

The company, founded in 1919 as the Campbell Cereal Company, was moved to Northfield in 1927. Earning the name Malt-O-Meal in 1953, the plant's hot wheat cereal has, as its motto proudly proclaims, "warmed the hearts and souls of America" for generations.

Northfield was founded in 1855 on the banks of the Cannon River by attorney John W. North and blacksmith/farmer I. S. Field. The Cannon, which flows 100 miles from Shields Lake to Red Wing, is part of Minnesota's Wild and Scenic

River system. The French called the stretch of smooth water "the river of canoes," and today's sports lovers can do the same. As cultivation developed in the 1850s, several other towns were built along the river to service the milling needs of the community. At one time, land speculators almost outnumbered the farmers. Three water-powered mills in Northfield churned out upwards of 3,000 barrels of flour a day, at $2 a barrel, a princely sum in the eastern cities.

The wheat market collapsed in the 1870s and at least fifteen mills along the Cannon fell into disrepair. Even the most eagle-eyed canoeist will find it hard to locate any crumbling foundations amid the cottonwoods lining the riverbanks. All the towns that the developers promoted at $100 a frontage foot are long gone, as well. Most were plowed under.

It's more relaxing these days in Northfield than on September 7, 1876, when Jesse James and his gang paid a visit to the local First National Bank. The desperadoes were "inquiring about a withdrawal" that would have included a recent deposit by mill owner Ames. There must have been some confusion over the names of respective Jesses because a gun battle erupted in which a bank teller and a Swedish immigrant were killed. Two members of the James gang were also sent to the Great Holdup in the Sky. Bullet holes can still be seen in the front wall of the bank, now a museum and homebase for the Northfield Historical Society. An M&M candy machine sits just inside the front door; for five cents, a visitor can get a handful of the goodies that melt in your mouth, not in your hand.

Up to 1,000 townsfolk chased the bandits out of town, capturing the gang's Younger brothers in a marsh north of Madelia, some fifty miles west of Northfield. The James boys themselves made a clean getaway by another route, sans money, to far-off South Dakota. Yet with revisionist history the rage these days, they'd probably be welcomed back to

FIRST NATIONAL BANK

The James Gang poses before the ill-fated First National Bank

play a leading role in the Defeat of Jesse James Days, a community pageant traditionally held the weekend following Labor Day.

Whoop-n-holler festivities include a reenactment of the raid, complete with galloping horses, blazing pistols, and scurrying townsfolk in appropriate costume. Then there's a spine-jerking rodeo, a beard-judging competition, a monster tractor pull, an arts fest, and a blazing carnival midway.

An antique red popcorn wagon perches in Bridge Park, called Horsecollar Park in the old days. Scents of hot, buttery popping corn emanate from the stand, which fronts the cream-colored brick bank/museum near a monument to the town's Civil War veterans. The wagon's operator, Wayne ("just call me Sherwin") Sherwin churns out "tons and tons" of popcorn each summer, he says. The wagon, built in 1918, is the retired oil jobber's home away from home from May through October. Thursday nights are the busiest, when there are strolling musicians and other performers in the Square.

One wonders what Jesse (James or Ames) would think of the rollerblader in his emerald-green fluorescent tights whizzing down the Fourth Street hill. Thighs pumping, he rushes past the stop sign at the foot of the bluff without a pause, whips around the war memorial, and swoops over the Cannon River before disappearing around a far corner with the clackety-clack of wheels.

Head north out of town on Division Street (State 3), past the Blue Monday Coffeehouse, where there's usually a few good ol' boys perched on benches out front on sunny days. Turn right on Northfield Boulevard (County 47), which used to be an Indian trail. Pause at the memorial on the left side of the road marking the Pioneer Wheat Trail and reflect on the wagon trains that used to pass by on their way to Hastings and the giant mills there. The old wheat road to Hastings is clearly marked by signs. Where oxen and mules once trod, trucks downshift around the curves and roar over the hills.

About five miles up County 47, turn right on Cannon River Boulevard (actually a gravel road that parallels the river) for a closer look at the fountain-like irrigation sprays watering the fields. Tens of thousands of gallons over the course of a summer ensure a ready corn crop, regardless of rainfall. Take Cannon River to the T-intersection with Alta Avenue and turn left to get back on County 47. You'll come out at the highway just across from the William Offe farm, with its three towering blue silos and contented Holsteins milling around the feedlot. With their white-and-black coats, the cows are as formal as conventioneers at a cocktail reception.

Next on the route is the village of Hampton, where prosperous-appearing St. Mathias Church is the principal landmark. But Lucky's Roundup Bar on Main Street, with its front windows vibrantly flashing with Schmidt and Grain Belt beer signs, and the nearby Frank's Place do another kind of booming business. However, farms in the area sport "Milk for Health" signs amid the asparagus fields.

Even from a vantage point miles south of Hastings, you'll spot the storage towers of the Con Agra mill above the prairie. An Avalon, this temple to the wheat industry remains one of North America's largest grinding plants. Sprawling over several acres at the junction of US 61 and County 47, ranks of holding bins, rail lines, parked trucks, and weigh stations are testimony to the fertility of Minnesota and points west.

Formerly Oliver's Grove, named after Lt. William Oliver, whose Fort Snelling supply boat was stuck in the ice here in 1819, Hastings rests at the convergence of the St. Croix, Vermillion, and Mississippi rivers. In 1853, the town was renamed Hastings, after the middle name of Henry H. Sibling, Minnesota's first governor.

The Vermillion still roars over a falls where today's plant was built in bits and pieces around the old mill wheel, which is now part of the basement. Con Agra took over the plant from King Midas Flour in 1983, adding the facility to its other twenty-eight mills from Utah to Buffalo. A little park provides a good view of the roaring falls, with its seventy-five-foot drop across the river from the grain elevators. A better look at the falls is secured from behind the mill, but that vantage point is off-limits to the public.

The milling byproducts, such as wheat hulls and seed kernels, are used for cattle feed. The flour is hauled to Duluth for shipping out on the Great Lakes to points east.

Standing in the parking lot in the shadow of those towers and talking with maintenance worker Elmo Martin, a passerby could get a strained neck bending back to look at those sky-stabbing pinnacles. Martin, who has worked at the plant for more than thirty years, takes it all in stride. His scuffed and battered hard hat, labeled with a faded Peavey Co. logo, hunkers low on his brow. He snacks on Old Dutch potato chips during a break.

Weigher Marshall Stein, a twenty-six-year veteran, takes a second for a chat. He comes out of his scale shed to rattle off some figures. Statistically, the mill can be mind-boggling. Annually, upwards of 17 million bushels of wheat and rye from Montana, the Dakotas, Minnesota, and other states flow through the silos, which are sixty to eighty feet tall and capable of holding 26,000 to 32,000 bushels each. Every gray Soo Line railroad car that pulls into the weighing area contains at least 3,300 bushels. In addition, Wayne Buesing's monster trucks and those of other haulers churn into the holding areas to wait in long lines for their turn to unload. Every truck carries at least 750 bushels, with every bushel weighing sixty pounds.

Within the complex are five mills: two for hard wheat, able to grind twenty-five bushels a minute; one for durham wheat, grinding twelve bushels a minute for the rich flour used for pasta; one rye mill; and one specialty mill for whole wheat, pumpernickel, or other type of flour. This "smaller" mill can grind 2.5 bushels a minute. The operation goes twenty-four hours a day, 350 days out of the year. That's a lot of pie crust—at least 2.5 million pounds of flour a day.

A visit to the Alexis Bailly winery is imperative when visiting Hastings. Southeastern Minnesota's only vineyard is about two miles east on US 61, reached by taking 170th Street to Kirby Road. The latter is gravel surfaced, so drive slowly the quarter mile it takes to reach the entrance drive. Rank after rank of hardy vines mark the twelve-acre property.

As Baron Phillippe de Rothschild remarked, "To develop character, great wines must go through hardship. Snow. Drought. Storms. There must be suffering to produce it."

He must have had Minnesota wine in mind. Bailly's hardy entrants have overcome knee-deep drifts and subzero temperatures to produce vintages that have won in the Eastern Wine Competition International and earned praise from the American Wine Society.

The winery is open from noon to 5:00 P.M. Friday through Sunday from mid-May to October. It's great fun to be there on opening weekend, listening to Minneapolis jazz pianist Drew Gordon and his combo. Bring friends for congenial sipping of ruby Marechal Foch or to sample the dry crispness of the Axel Bailly Seyval Blanc. The best place to be on a warm afternoon weekend is in the breezy, cool comfort of a vine-shrouded patio. It's all so . . . so . . . continental.

The original Alexis Bailly was an early pioneer who emigrated to the Hastings area from Quebec. He was the great-grandfather of the current operators: Nan, Susan, and John Bailly. Their father, David, a prominent Minneapolis attorney, bought the land in 1972 and began the plantings in 1973. "It was a real family affair," asserts Susan, who coordinates marketing and runs the tastings. Sister Nan is the winemaker. Brother John manages the vineyard itself, assisted in the picking of grapes by a Hmong family that lives nearby and numerous wine-loving volunteers from the Twin Cities.

The Baillys have worked closely with the University of Minnesota to develop tough strains of vines, able to withstand Minnesota's legendary cold and snow. Hard work has paid off. The Bailly family now produces about 3,000 cases of assorted reds and whites each year. That's about 5,000 gallons, sold mostly in trendy Twin Cities restaurants and upscale wine shops.

Return to the main highway and the drive back to Hastings. This comfortable river town shows its farm heritage with the Anson Brothers Grain Co. silos at 2nd and Main streets near the rolling river and on the west wall of the Macro-Bar at the other end of downtown. There, artist Sheila Graham painted an old-time packet steamer, reminiscent of those that used to haul freight back and forth from the Twin Cities. The town's burgher-stolid prosperity shows up in its architecture. The 1863 Meyer Building, 1880 Finch Building, and the 1895 Griffin Building proudly carry their dates and titles carved in stone high above the sidewalks.

Park and stroll along the Veterans Memorial Levee, where an original rope-pulled ferryboat carried passengers. The ferry ceased operations when the first bridge was built in 1895. A giant granite boulder behind the American Legion Post stands as a memorial to the town's war dead. An American flag snaps in the breeze there, alongside a black POW remembrance flag.

Hastings is a maple-shaded town of porches. A welcome overnight at the Thorwood Inn at Fourth and Pine streets is preceded by a chat in the cool afternoon with owner Pam Thorsen. "There are real treasures around here," she says, discussing the historical preservation efforts made by many of her neighbors. Sixty-two homes are registered historical landmarks, many of them earmarked through the efforts of Hazel Johnson, a local historian and close friend of Thorsen and her husband, Dick.

The Thorsens' bed and breakfast has variously been a private home, a hospital, and then a rooming house. It is only one of dozens highlighted on a walking tour around town. And, for real front-porch fans, there's always the Hastings Front Porch Festival in May—complete with maypole dancing and parades.

From Hastings, there are numerous backroad jaunts to take for an exploration of the Mississippi River valley. One especially good road is County 54 through the Gores Pool State Wildlife Management Area east of town. And that is saved for another Country Roads drive.

In the Area

Northfield Area Chamber of Commerce (Northfield):
507-645-5604 or 800-658-2548

Northfield Historical Society Bank Museum (Northfield):
507-645-9268

Malt-O-Meal Co. (Northfield): 507-645-6681

Alexis Bailly Vineyard (Hastings): 612-437-1413

Thorwood Historic Inns (Hastings): 612-437-3297

Hastings Chamber of Commerce (Hastings): 612-437-6775

Carpenter St. Croix Valley Nature Center (Hastings):
612-437-4359

25

3 ~

Mantorville-
St. Peter

Getting There: From the Twin Cities, take I-35 south to State 60 and turn east to State 57. At Wanamingo, turn south to Mantorville.

Highlights: *Civil War-era buildings, state parks, stagecoach towns, colleges, art galleries, antique shops, buffalo herds, scenic overlooks, historic main streets.*

Looking for stagecoaches in the flatlands of southern Minnesota is like seeking Mayan temples in the steaming jungles of Chiapas. You know they were there once in abundance, but finding one today is difficult. One coach can be spotted in Racine, about twenty miles south of Rochester, parked jauntily back from US 63 near the entrance of the 7th Rib Restaurant. But other than that old wagon, no others are to be seen outside a museum. But dozens would have been readily in sight during the state's rough and rugged frontier days.

In those pre-train-auto-bus-airplane days, the familiar Wells Fargo coaches or open wagons fitted with planks for seats and "passenger buggies" rattled their way from village to village throughout most of lower Minnesota. They delivered passengers, mail, and other freight—all democratically coated with the same dust or mud—through twenty-some years of the state's dramatic population explosion after becoming a territory.

From the late 1840s to just before the Civil War, stage roads were the main transportation arteries. Yet cutting through forests, across prairieland, and over rolling hills was always a challenge. Potholes seemed large enough to swallow an entire team. Saplings and tree trunks were cut to fill in wet spots. Pick-and-shovel labor sometimes smoothed the bumpier tracks, but not always. Occasionally, it was safer for the fare-paying passengers to walk rather than risk whiplash.

But as one accomplished driver noted, "If ya kin see daylight between the trees, ya kin git through."

These crude roads were the pathways to what was hoped would be fame and fortune for nervous new immigrants, for salesmen making their rounds, for theater companies bringing culture, and for gamblers, buskers, and hustlers of all stripes. Many contemporary highways now follow the route of those first rough coach roads. Today, whizzing along US 14 or County 16, it is easy to forget what those early Minnesotans endured just to get from place to place.

The stagecoach got its name from the fact that the coach made its journey in stages. About every fifteen miles, the coachman changed horses to ensure "speedy" trips on the long rides between communities. One of the first established runs, a daily wagon line between St. Paul and St. Anthony, kicked off in 1849. That trip was noted for being served by grizzled teamsters whose cussword vocabulary was considered extraordinary in a profession admired for its creative elocution. The verbiage was not simply colorful, it was Technicolored and rainbow-hued, much to the consternation of elderly widows, preachers, and genteel *femmes* who were passengers.

Rice and Myrick, "stage proprietors and livery stable keepers," operated from the rear of St. Paul's American House hotel, the city's primary depot for the daily 8:00 A.M. and 2:00 P.M. trips to St. Anthony. On Wednesdays, an 8:00 A.M. run was made to Fort Ripley. In 1855, the company trumpeted that "having made large additions to our stock, we are enabled to furnish Horses and Vehicles in style and 'getting up,' equal to any establishment of the kind in the United States."

In the early 1850s, Stillwater was served three times a week by a stage line to St. Paul. It was probable that golden-tongued, flamboyant, tobacco-chawing teamsters on that route were just as admired by impressionable young boys as they were abhorred by their mothers.

Even Minnesota's legendary winters were not considered enough to halt the increasing amounts of overland traffic. For instance, sleighs were used between St. Paul and Galena, Illinois. Sometimes, drivers had to wade into the drifts ahead of their teams to help break through snowy barricades. Buffalo-skin robes and hot bricks on the coach floors kept frost-edged passengers from shivering and shaking out of their hard seats.

Martin O. Walker, who owned stage lines throughout the Midwest, began operating in Minnesota in 1854. Bringing extensive experience from developing routes through Iowa, Missouri, and Illinois, he established the first consistent service linking St. Paul with Dubuque, Iowa. Walker was an all-around transportation mogul. He built his own roads, hired his own drivers, subcontracted construction of the coaches, provided box lunches, and established rest stops. However, according to the Minnesota Historical Society, one upset passenger was not impressed with Walker's entrepreneurial expertise. The man wrote that he wished "Walker might forever be driven around the gloomy bogs and swamps of Hades by his saucy drivers, in his rickety stages, behind his skeleton horse frames."

Competition was not far behind. In 1856, James C. Burbank set up the Northwestern Express Company to provide transportation between St. Paul and Prairie du Chien, Wisconsin. He eventually ran a coach to Dubuque. Burbank's Northwestern Express Company became the Minnesota Stage Company in 1859, soon operating about 1,300 miles of routes.

At first, the stagecoach companies used military trails. But, as in the case of Walker and his rivals, it was easier to construct private roads. Whenever two lines crisscrossed or forded a river, a tavern or hotel would spring up, planting the seeds for a town.

During the heyday of the coach lines, just before the 1870s brought the relatively faster, cleaner, and easier-on-the-derriere railroads, the main routes extended from Breckenridge on the Dakota border to Winona on the Mississippi River. Major hubs were Rochester, Owatonna, St. Peter, Faribault, Mendota, St. Cloud, and St. Paul.

To learn more about the establishment of the state's coach roads, read Arthur J. Larson's *The Development of Minnesota's Road System* (Minnesota Historical Society, 1966) or Grover Singley's *Tracing Minnesota's Old Government Roads* (Minnesota Historical Society, 1974).

One of the best places to start a modern "stagecoach" tour on Minnesota's country roads is historic Mantorville, twelve miles west of Rochester. Since 1854, the Hubbell House has been a rest stop for travelers. Located at 5th and Main streets, the first structure was a two-story log tavern and hotel, considered the first public lodging establishment in Minnesota. That building was torn down in 1857 by owner J. B. Hubbell, who then built the existing stone hotel. Although he served several times as County sheriff, Hubbell had to leave town shortly after fixing up the hotel, allegedly owing a great deal of money. The word was that he "went fishing and disappeared." Supposedly, he was killed by a bear somewhere out in the Wild West.

Through a succession of subsequent owners, the Hubbell House fell into disrepair. It was rescued and renovated in 1946 by Rochester restaurateur Paul Pappas, who saw plenty of possibilities behind the crumbling facade. Son Don now runs the restaurant, which has kept up the long-standing tradition of catering to coach tours as well as serving the drop-in traveler. Carved on the wooden boardwalk around the front of the building are names of visitors from Connecticut, Texas, Missouri, and other states. Because of its prime location, the village was one of the major stops on the east-west trace between Rochester and Owatonna. Among the more famous visitors to the Hubbell House in its early years were U. S. Grant, Gen. William T. Sherman, and famed Norwegian violinist Ole Bull. Later, under the Pappas mantle, President Dwight D. Eisenhower, magician Fred Blackstone, and circus impresario John Ringling North were among those who enjoyed eating there.

As Paul Pappas said, "Give folks the steak and seafood they like and they'll park their Cadillacs, Lincolns, Volkswagens, Chevrolets, Fords, and Plymouths outside your door in such numbers that soon you'll have to build an addition to your supper club." Add "stagecoach" to the list.

Located at the junction of County 16 and State 57, Mantorville is about three miles north of Kasson. By the turn of the century, the building of a rail depot helped Kasson eclipse its smaller northern neighbor, although Mantorville remained the Dodge County seat. The paving of what is now the east-west US 14 through Kasson also impeded Mantorville's growth.

Yet an influx of young, upward-bound residents after World War II reversed the downward trend. Seeking affordable homes, living space, and a family environment, they flocked to the countryside, where it was an easy commute to the major cities nearby. With that energy, historic downtown Mantorville buildings were restored in the 1950s and 1960s after years of neglect. The tuck-pointing, cleanup-fixup campaign turned the brick Mantorville Merchantile Exchange and other buildings into photo postcard places. In the autumn, when crimson and orange maples fire-rocket the side streets with their brilliance, Mantorville comes even more alive with all the tourists.

Mantorville city clerk Ann Wilke remembers exploring the banks of the Zumbro River as a child in the 1930s, when rutted stagecoach tracks across the fords could still be seen. She hands out fliers on historic Mantorville in the city hall office, a low 1960ish building adjacent to the firehouse on 5th Street.

Portions of that original trail remain. Leaving the Hubbell House, drive north on State 57 and turn left (west) onto 7th Street. Then take a right onto Jefferson Street just beyond the ballpark. Drive past the Pioneer Trails housing development, and you'll be back on the original old coach trace. Graveled and bumpy, the country road takes you into the backdoor of tiny Wasioja, a drive of about three dusty, curving miles. The road parallels the Zumbro, a muddy stream noted for its excellent bullhead fishing and swimming holes, protected as they are by shady willows perfect for kid-swinging. It's easy to imagine riding a coach over the same route fifteen decades ago.

Wasioja was founded in 1856, with dreams of grandeur never quite realized, because the town was bypassed by the railroad. A Methodist seminary there remained open until the 1890s, serving young men from throughout the vicinity. Many of them were among the 200-plus soldiers from the town and surrounding farms who marched off to the Civil War as starry-eyed grunts in Company C, 2nd Minnesota

Volunteers. They had signed up at a small stone building that was once the town bank but had been turned into a recruiting station.

The seminary was destroyed by arsonists in 1905. Its foundation is almost hidden by towering pine trees planted as striplings after the Civil War. The trees were to memorialize those local men who died bloodily screaming at Chickamauga and other battles. The young warriors of Company C distinguished themselves after quickly losing their innocence. A state historical society plaque outside the ruins keeps the memory of the building and its long-ago residents alive. The recruiting center still stands, the only one remaining in the state. Surrounded by a protective chain-link fence, the building seems so small considering its important place in Minnesota's history. The rattle of drums and squeal of fifes still hang on the late summer air if you listen carefully enough.

Wasioja's other touches with fame include the formation of Minnesota's first Baptist congregation. When the denomination's church was dedicated in 1861, elder W. C. Shepard walked nine miles from Ashland in fifty-degree-below-zero temperatures to hear a Rochester preacher shake the shingles with a hellfire sermon. That church is gone now, as are many of the other buildings in what used to be a thriving farm community.

Leaving Wasioja, aim west on State 16, cross State 56 to Dodge County G, and pick up Steele County 19 at Rice Lake, where it joins with County 20. All that remains of the pioneer village of Rice Lake at that site is a little white church, not far from the entrance to Rice Lake State Park. County 19 will then wend its way into the east side of Owatonna, sixty miles south of Minneapolis-St. Paul.

Rice Lake State Park, about seven miles east of Owatonna, contains remnants of vegetation that made up a vast oak savanna thousands of years ago. Called the Southern Oak Barrens, the stretch of trees and prairie once covered 7 percent of Minnesota: from what is now the Twin Cities to the far western prairies and east to the forests along the Mississippi River. Settlers plowed up most of this region, but a strip around an old cemetery at the east end of the park was spared over generations of encroaching farm sites. It is now one of the rarest parcels of original prairieland and oak left in the state. Camping, picnicking, fishing, and hiking here provide plenty of outdoor options. In addition, Rice Lake State Park is enough to drive a bird fancier nuts. Seven species of woodpecker, plus whistling swans, blue geese, and dozens of other birds can be spotted. The thick rat-a-tat-tat of a pileated woodpecker resounds through the park, as if someone dumped marbles on a steel drumhead. The crow-size bird must be scrounging for carpenter ants in one of the park's fallen trees.

Speaking of food . . . the first thing you should do upon arriving in Owatonna is eat lunch at The Kitchen, located at Rose and Cedar streets. There's nothing fancy here, just solid Upper Midwest food such as turkey noodle hot dish, thick bean soup, and homemade pie (sour cream raspberry, lemon delight, Dutch apple, and cherry, among other sinful selections). The apple crunch is the most dangerous item on the pie chart, posted daily with whatever confections stellar piemaker Debbie Sorg feels like producing that day. The whipped cream atop the crunch is the crowning caloric glory. In the background, folks in Owatonna bowling league jackets chat about who's laid up in the hospital that week.

One wonders if the long-ago guests at the nearby old Arnold Hotel, once a stagecoach stop and now a fancy floral shop, had such good lunch fixin's and breezy conversation. They probably did. After all, this IS Minnesota, the state that invented The Hot Dish. The Arnold was erected in 1866 and served as a hotel until September of 1983.

The city is named after an Indian woman, Owatonna, who was treated at the warm, bubbly springs in the center of what is now the city's east-side Mineral Springs Park. A statue of Owatonna is the main focus in the maple-shaded park. Tribes from around the region appreciated the value of the *minnewaucan* (curing water), and many early pioneers praised the springs for their purity, located as they are near Maple Creek. To see for yourself, take Mineral Springs Road from downtown to Mineral Springs Parkway and the park entrance.

The imposing red brick of the National Farmers' Bank Building, designed by famed architect Louis Sullivan, anchors the downtown. The bank, now called Norwest Bank Owatonna, was completed in 1908. At the time, according to legend, Sullivan's business had slumped, so he was glad to get a call about the job from bank manager Carl Bennett. Sullivan did such great work that his reputation was revitalized. Peek into the lobby (folks are friendly in Owatonna so they don't mind) and look over the 200 shades of color he used in the interior design. The electric chandeliers weigh two and a quarter tons each. Sullivan wanted the locals to be impressed—and they certainly were. Even when the bill was paid.

The Village of Yesteryear, a collection of ten historic buildings collected by the Steele County Historical Society, is a valuable stop for anyone pursuing stagecoach history. Curator Marlene Knutson rummages through the archives in the Dunnell House, the main building in the complex, to come up with historical tidbits about the coach lines and their personnel. She finds one faded clipping about Jacob Jorgenson, a German immigrant who was born in 1855, coming to Owatonna in 1882. Jorgenson drove stagecoaches and mail wagons between Owatonna and Albert Lea for years. The undated news story, however, focused on one sad side note: Jorgenson's suicide.

On a more upbeat note, local resident Betty Johnson, who lives on a farm twelve miles south of town on County 7, remembers her mother-in-law telling of the four-horse teams that used to roll past her family's home. Often, the battered stages would stop at the nearby Hanson house, where the loose-jointed passengers would get a cool drink of water before moving on into Owatonna, she recalls.

The Village of Yesteryear, located on the Steele County fairgrounds along 18th Street S.E., is open from 1:00 to 5:00 P.M. daily from May 1 to September 30. Admission is $2 for individuals, $5 for a family, and $1 per student. The village is perfectly manageable for a family stroll, especially when you're attending an event at the fairgrounds. In addition to the Dunnell House, built by the only Owatonna resident to serve in Congress, there is a railroad station kidnapped from the village of Bixby, the St. Wenceslaus of Moravia Catholic Church, a schoolhouse, and assorted other buildings straight from the pages of the county's early history.

From the history village complex, take Lincoln Avenue south across US 218 and 14 to Nechville's Buffalo Farm, about three miles south of town on Route 4 (County 6). On the way to the buffalo farm is the Bohemian National Cemetery, visible on the east side of the road. A monument out front tells that the site was established in 1856. Bordered by pines, the plot is now the final resting place for the Veselys, Chmeliks, Soubas, and Horaks. Only the soughing of Corn Country wind through the trees and the far-off roar of semis on the highway mark a contemporary hymn for the pioneers buried here. For any detailed information about the cemetery or the Czech, Slovak, and Moravian people who settled around Owatonna, call Don Seykora (705-451-5125), Gerald Souba (705-451-2065), or Eloise Maixner (705-451-4745).

But back to the buffalo. Turn right at the first gravel road beyond the cemetery, about one-quarter mile south of US 218/14. The shaggy animals are seen in a farm pen, looking slow and lumpy under their furry humps like a poker party of bachelor great-uncles. From the driveway, you are about as close as you would ever want to be these Lords of the Plains. And yes . . . they do smell.

35

Visit Nechville's Buffalo Farm

If you ever have the opportunity to prepare buffalo meat for supper, Don Nechville has some tips. "There is no such thing as tough buffalo meat. There are only improperly instructed cooks," says a flier he hands out at the farm. By the "weigh," there are only fifty calories per ounce in buffalo meat, making it an acceptable alternative to beef in any diet plan. Here is a recipe for buffalo roast, courtesy of the National Buffalo Association, of which Nechville is a member:

> 3- or 4-pound buffalo roast
> 1 slice bacon, cut into small pieces
> 2 cloves garlic, crushed
> salt and pepper
> 1 bay leaf
> 2 cloves
> 1 cup orange juice

Cut slits in meat and insert small pieces of bacon and garlic. Salt and pepper well. Sear meat on all sides. Put meat in roaster and place bay leaf and cloves on top. Baste with orange juice. Roast in 325-degree oven until internal temperature reaches 170 degrees, basting frequently.

But don't forget that you first have to catch the buffalo before you can have a buffalo roast. Or give Nechville a call at 507-451-3765 to find an easier way. The National Buffalo Association can also tell you of the closest buffalo-meat supplier. Contact the organization at P.O. Box 580, Fort Pierre, SD 57531. 606-223-2829.

Leaving the buffalo behind (a rump steak trip?), continue west from Owatonna on US 14 to Mankato, again part of an old-time stagecoach run. The forty-two-mile drive is quick and easy, unlike the good old times when a stage journey would take almost two days. Midway between both cities is

Janesville, where a row of multicolored grain storage bins on the west side of town spells out the town name.

While driving through Mankato, stop at the Minnesota Valley Regional Library, 100 East Main Street, for a look through the Maud Hart Lovelace collection. The noted local author wrote the delightful Betsy/Tacy series of children's books, and many of her original notes and other memorabilia are on display. A slide-tape presentation tells of her life in Mankato. The collection is open from 9:30 A.M. to 8:00 P.M. Monday through Thursday and from 9:30 A.M. to 5:00 P.M. on Friday and Saturday.

Mankato is justifiably proud of it arts heritage, with a community orchestra and the Highland Summer Theater and the Conkling Art Gallery, both located at Mankato State University.

Turn north in Mankato onto State 22 to St. Peter, located at a major crossing on the Minnesota River. The city, founded in 1853, is one of the oldest in the state and was a major hub on the coach lines that crisscrossed this corner of Minnesota. The city's small brick tourism center is in Levee Park, on State 99 one block east of the junction with US 169 and State 22. Youngsters under sixteen and the young-at-heart over sixty-five can fish in the river behind the center. The St. Peter Food Co-op is across the street, offering fresh apple cider (in season) for a mere $3.99 a gallon. A swig of the cider offers a delightfully tantalizing mix of tartness and sweetness.

The St. Peter river crossing, Traverse des Sioux, was long known to Native Americans and the French trappers who followed in their footsteps. A trading post at the crossing, just north of the current city of 10,000, was the locale where an 1851 treaty was signed with the Dakota Sioux, ceding 24 million acres of land to the federal government. Almost before the ink was dry on the beribboned parchment, a group of businessmen formed the St. Peter Company for the purpose of developing the town site. They hoped to make their community the state capital instead of St. Paul. A wide main street (Minnesota Avenue, of course) was laid out in anticipation of being given the nod. However, Joe Rolette, a rival legislator who was opposed to the change, stole the bill that would have made the switch. The governor then signed authorization verifying St. Paul as the capital, so St. Peter lost the crown.

Yet that affair was eventually forgotten, and five residents of St. Peter went on to become governors of Minnesota, including John A. Johnson, who was the first native-born Minnesotan to occupy the current state capitol building.

Until the mid-1860s, the stagecoaches linked St. Peter to the Twin Cities, the river towns along the Mississippi, the farm communities in the west, and Iowa to the south. The Nicollet Hotel, 124 South Minnesota, was famed for the travelers it accommodated over those early years, ranging from bandit Jesse James to politician William Jennings Bryan. Another thirteen buildings in the city are on the National Register of Historic Places. The Julien Cox House, 500 North Washington Street, was once the center of the pioneer town's lively social whirl and is now open for tours hosted by costumed interpreters. Admission is $1.50.

But progress did not play any favorites. The St. Peter *Tribune* in October of 1868 lamented the passing of the stagecoaches, as railroads took over. The paper said sadly, "The old pioneers disappeared before the commodious and speedy vehicles demanded by the enlarging population and trade."

The Nicollet County Historical Society, however, doesn't want all that to be forgotten. A new museum opened in 1994, on the site of the treaty with the Sioux in Traverse des Sioux Park along US 169. With 14,500 square feet of exhibit space and a research library in which to work, society director John Haus is a happy man.

When you stand in the park along the banks of the slowly rolling Minnesota River, with the cry of crows in the

*Everyone from William Jennings Bryan to Jesse James
stayed at the Nicollet Hotel*

far-off woods, the past never seems far away. And is that a rumbling knock of stagecoach wheels in the distance?

Naw, it can't be.

Or is it?

In the Area

State Historic Preservation Office, Minnesota Historical Society: 612-726-1171

Mantorville Chamber of Commerce (Mantorville): 507-635-2331

Owatonna Visitors and Convention Bureau (Owatonna): 800-423-6466

Owatonna Arts Center (Owatonna): 507-451-4540

Village of Yesteryear (Owatonna): 507-451-1329

Conkling Art Gallery, Mankato State University: 507-389-6412

Highland Summer Theatre, Mankato State University: 507-389-6661

Julien Cox House (St. Peter): 507-931-21060

St. Peter Area Chamber of Commerce (St. Peter): 800-473-3404

Treaty Site History Center (St. Peter): 507-931-2160

4 ~

Red Wing-
La Crescent

Getting there: From the Twin
Cities, take US 52 south, turning east on State 50 at Hampton. State 50 widens to the
four-lane US 61 just before
you arrive at Red Wing, about
an hour from Minneapolis-St.
Paul. From Red Wing, it's
about ninety miles south on
US 61 to La Crescent.

Highlights: *apple orchards and
pumpkin patches, scenic overlooks, steamboat towns, bike
trails, museums, and exceptional
eateries.*

Ol' man river, he jes keeps rollin' along. Past turn-of-the-
century river towns, under interstate bridges, over shifting
sandbars, around muskrat houses, and along stone-wall
levees, the muscular Mississippi River hums and rambles
southward along Minnesota's eastern borders.

Words from the famous song drift along the current, as
autumn fireworks pop and crackle in a fiery potpourri of oak
and maple, with yellowing birch and cottonwood accented by
crimson sumac. The waterfall of color dazzles the senses during the rush down steep hillsides to the Hershey-colored
river.

A jaunt south along US 61 is best during the fall Colorama. October's roadside fruit stands overflow with the tempting combination of plump red apples, giant pumpkins, and sweet honey. Towboats make their last run to ports downriver, pushing heavily loaded barges before winter's ice halts the commercial rush. On the opposite Wisconsin shore, other motorists are also enjoying some autumn meandering along the famous Great River Road (US 35).

The river valley is a flyway for Canada geese. They honk a seasonal farewell on their airy interstate route to marshy condos down south, leaving the skies to circling turkey vultures, red-winged hawks, and the occasional bald eagle. Deer creep around the evening edge of dying cornfields, nibbling harvest remainders. Raccoons, possums, and other low-hung critters scurry across the back roads on last-minute errands. Some are luckily quick and some are not so fortunate in confronting the traffic.

An autumn drive encourages browsing through antique shops, kicking leaves in state parks, snuggling under quilts in small-town bed and breakfasts, sampling apple cider, and licking fingers sticky with fresh caramel. Subsequently, this Minnesota riverway sampler rates a 10 on the Country Roads Expedition Scale.

This can be a day trip or a long weekend or more, depending, of course, on one's inclination to dawdle, dream, and nibble apple slices. Since it is only about an hour's drive south of the Twin Cities, an expedition of any length can be fun without being tiring. There are also plenty of opportunities for side excursions. So hone the scouting instinct and hit the road.

For instance, twelve miles northwest of Red Wing and two miles south of US 61 on County 7, Welch Mill outfitters have rentals and shuttles for canoeing and tubing (cold in October!) along the Cannon River through the Richard J. Dorer Memorial Hardwood Forest. There are also nineteen excellent miles of hiking and biking opportunities on the paved Cannon Valley Trail through rural Goodhue County between Cannon Falls and Red Wing. No motorized vehicles are allowed, but each person sixteen and older using wheels on the route (bikes, skates, and so on) needs a $2 wheel pass from April through October. The passes can be secured from the Outdoor Store, 323 Main Street, at Nybo's Landing (a bowling alley and restaurant located at 233 Withers Harbor Drive) or at the trailheads. A recorded phone message at the Welch Trail Station provides updates on riding conditions. Call 507-258-4567. Folks at the Red Wing City Hall, 507-263-3954, can also answer questions.

Yet if nature needs a backseat break, try the Treasure Island Casino and Bingo Parlor, fifteen miles north of Red Wing. Look for the signs along US 61 that will lead to Las Vegas-style gambling run by local Mdewakanton Sioux. One thousand glittering slots and fifty-two blackjack tables lure the passerby with promises of riches on a twenty-four-hour-a-day basis. At the nearby tribal community on Prairie Island, there is a marina and recreational vehicle park. Take winding County 18 north off US 61.

Almost a mandatory first stop on this seasonal sojourn is the Red Wing Stoneware outlet on the eastern fringe of Red Wing. Easily spotted on the north side of US 61, the modern workshop and retail outlet is the contemporary heir apparent to the old Red Wing Pottery Works. In 1984, owner and potter John Falconer revived the tradition that made the community famous since the last century. With his bib overalls, trademark straw hat, and Falstaffian beard, Falconer's presence is always noticeable. Visitors to the pottery can watch the "throwing" of clay, the actual pot-making process, through windows opening onto the workroom.

Antique aficionados will find themselves in heaven along Old Main Street, unofficially tagged "Antique Alley." Shops overflowing with collectibles are located in homes and warehouses along the street that leads into the historic manufacturing district. Fifty-two dealerships and factory outlets are housed in the formidable main plant of the original Red Wing Pottery Works, now on the National Register of Historic Places. The company was shut down in 1967 after a long and bitter strike, but its jugs and mugs remain collector's items. Upwards of 3,000 pottery packrats who love the traditional stoneware come to Red Wing each July for a convention and gabfest.

A reporter on the Red Wing *Daily Republican* was dead-on when he wrote on October 5, 1893, that a "scene more beautiful than an autumn sunset up the river can scarcely be imagined, and it will repay the lover of nature to take a skiff some pleasant, clear evening and behold what an enchanting scene it is . . ." Today's traveler doesn't necessarily need to park along Levee Road and look for a rowboat to sample the season's enchantment.

You'll find a great view of the city and the Mississippi on Sorin's Bluff, reached by car off 7th Street from downtown, through the stone gateway to Memorial Hill Drive. On the peak are picnic tables and walkways. Another overlook is atop Barn Bluff on the city's north side, with a hiking path up from 5th Street. A climber needs to be in fairly good condition for that steep incline, however.

The first whites settled in the area in 1837, near a Dakota Sioux farming village, and the town grew to be one of the major manufacturing and agricultural hubs on the upper Mississippi. Flour mills, shoe factories (yes, the famous Red Wing shoes are still made in the town), lime quarries, and furniture construction were the economic mainstays. Walking tours to observe the city's historic architecture offer an excellent way to sample the past. Simply follow the strolling suggestions laid out in a pamphlet provided by the Red Wing Area Chamber of Commerce and the Red Wing Heritage Preservation Commission. Most shops have the free fold-out flier for giving away.

The Sheldon Performing Arts Theatre at the corner of 3rd Street and East Avenue remains an entertainment jewel. Docent and board member Judy Christiansen leads fascinating tours regularly through the stately old building, built in 1904 as the nation's first municipal theater. It was refurbished after a fire in 1987. Minnesota artists are always featured in rotating lobby exhibitions, and a colorful audio-visual presentation located in an upstairs black-box theater presents the history of Red Wing and the theater.

Local actress Verna Frieka, portraying flamboyant hotelier Clara Nelson Lillyblad, often greets guests arriving at the ornate St. James Hotel, billed as "an elegant retreat in the Victorian tradition." Lillyblad came to work at the St. James in 1914, married the owner, and went on to manage the property until her death in 1972. Her son, Art, is now one of the hotel directors. An AAA Four Diamond property, it offers overnights from $75 to $145. Individually decorated and restored rooms are named after the powerful steamboats that plied the Mississippi River in the good old days. Each guest bed is covered in colorful Amish-style quilts made by Amos and Lydia Yoder of St. Charles, Minnesota.

A neat little paperback book, *If Walls Could Talk*, is a collection of reminiscences by the hotel staff. Complimentary copies are available in each room, making fun reading just before dozing off. There's one tale about circus performers who stayed overnight at the St. James after their car broke down. In the morning, the maids discovered that a dancing leopard had been smuggled into the room and was chained to a bathtub faucet. But that's a story for another time.

The luscious bread pudding concluding the hotel's Summit Restaurant Sunday brunch is fit for any passing king and queen. A warning—reservations are not taken for the 11:00 A.M. to 2:00 P.M. servings, but the wait is worth it.

A neat note: a third-floor kids' play area features antique-style toys such as tea sets, dolls, and rocking horses. A sad

note: a display in the nearby stairwell memoriali:
ninety-plus picnicking Red Wing residents who di‹
steamboat disaster on the river during the last century.

Frontenac State Park is next on the agenda, overlooking the murky waters where the aforementioned excursion
boat, the *Sea Wing,* capsized in a turbulent storm on July 13,
1890. Almost all aboard drowned in one of the river's worst
recorded boating catastrophes. The twenty-one-mile-long
Lake Pepin, where the Mississippi widens to three miles, now
lies calmly below the park ridgeline. Only the rustling of
crumbling brown maple leaves along the path whisper a dirge
for the deceased.

Also from the park bluffs at Point-No-Point, a visitor can
spot a spit of sand edging into the river that was believed to
be the site of a small French fort from the early 1700s. Leaving
the state park, a sharp-eyed driver can spot a herd of bison
lolling in the warm autumn sun. The shaggy beasts dot a
pasture across County 2 to the northwest. Run-of-the-mill
Holsteins are in an adjoining field, so don't confuse the two
types of ruminants.

The resort community of Frontenac is reached off dusty
Garrand Avenue from the highway. Mansions and cottages
are tucked into the thick riverfront groves, and, for some
reason, most of the homes are white with green shutters.
Frontenac had been one of the trendier places to be and to be
seen in during the river's whirlwind summer social season
at the turn of the century. However, some of the larger
old properties slid into disrepair as scions of the original Old
Money families from New Orleans and St. Louis changed
their lifestyle interests and moved on to other exotic locales
like Vail or St. Moritz. Yet life is slowly being breathed back
into many of the buildings as invading Twin Cities developers
move in with smiles, checkbooks, refurbishment plans, and
paintbrushes. There's more bustle now on the gravel side

streets and around the manicured lawns of the Villa Maria
retreat center, a former school and convent.

Typical of the new blood in the community, Michele
Hodgson, a writer for *Minneapolis-St. Paul* magazine, was recently married in the parlor of her father-in-law's house in
Frontenac. She and husband, Tom, the burly, mustachioed
swim coach at the University of St. Thomas in St. Paul,
immediately took a honeymoon houseboat cruise on the river.
They thereby enlivened the hamlet's fading image as a social/
vacation hub.

Lake City, five miles south of Frontenac, boasts an
expansive new marina and a midsummer Water Fest—which
is perfect, since the city proudly claims to be the birthplace of
waterskiing. In 1922, a local lad named Ralph Samuelson
strapped two thin boards on his feet, tied a rope behind a
friend's motorboat, and roared into history across Lake
Pepin's choppy waters. Suntanned Samuelson eventually
expanded his routine for awestruck vacationers, as he hung
onto a towrope tied to a seaplane and hopscotched over the
water. He took his show on the road, touring the country in
a yellow roadster. Once when a ski snapped during a perfor-
mance in Florida, he kept on going . . . and thus slalom skiing
was born. Young Samuelson eventually hung up his skis after
several injuries, returned home, and purchased a turkey
farm, fading into obscurity until the 1960s when a vacationing
St. Paul *Pioneer Press* reporter noticed his skis hanging in a
local bathhouse. She wrote a story and fame returned. Sets of
his skis are now hanging in the Minnesota Historical Society
collection in St. Paul and in the Lake City Chamber of Commerce office. A wave sculpture in Lake City's Ohuta Park
commemorates his accomplishments.

All that thinking about water skis works up an appetite,
which means a stop at the Chickadee Cottage Tea Room and
Restaurant, 317 North Lakeshore Drive, a self-proclaimed
"step back to homemade and leisurely." The Chickadee is

probably the only munch stop along US 61 where a motorist can indulge in a full English tea from 3:00 to 5:00 P.M. each afternoon. However, since tourist traffic slows in the winter, the restaurant is closed from the end of October until the end of April.

But bald eagles, not chickadees, have made the nearby fishing village of Reads Landing a worthwhile winter stop for travelers. Open water means lunch for the eagles, who feed on oxygen-starved fish that float near the surface between the ice chunks. Some inattentive ice fishermen have lost prize catches to the crafty feathered national emblems, which swoop down and pluck hard-earned catches from behind their backs.

The Anderson House in Wabasha is Minnesota's oldest operating hotel; it's included, of course, on the National Register of Historic Places. The antique-filled rooms even come equipped with a cat, if such is desired. Fred, Goblin, Tom-Tom, Aloysius, Morris, and their pals can be selected as overnight companions. Current owner John Shields Hall, the fourth generation of his family to run the red-brick hostel, started the well-publicized feline tradition after a long-ago hotel cat found its way into a guest's room and made himself at home. The visitor liked the domestic touch so much he told others and the word spread. There are some rooms off-limits to the friendly fuzzies, however, for folks with allergies.

Hall's great-grandmother, Ida Hoffman Anderson, purchased what was then the old Hurd House hotel in 1909. Her daughter, Verna, ran the hotel next, followed eventually by three granddaughters. Hall's mom, Jeanne McCaffrey Hall, went on to manage the Playboy Club mansion in Chicago in the early 1960s, which was "pretty heady stuff for a country girl," her son reported with a grin. Hall bought the hotel in 1978, laying on warm hospitality thick as the homemade mashed potatoes and gravy that grace his noteworthy open-face hot beef sandwiches.

The outgoing, ready-with-a-handshake hotel owner is also president of Mississippi Valley Partners, a loose tourist federation of twelve towns on the Minnesota and Wisconsin shores of Lake Pepin. The group recently initiated a record-breaking eighty-five-mile-long rummage sale during which all the communities laid out their basement, attic, and garage treasures. Over the holidays, each town "becomes" one of the twelve days of Christmas in another promotion designed to lure and keep visitors in the area.

The city has constructed an eagle-watching platform overlooking the river at Pembroke and Lawrence boulevards. Volunteers trained by the Raptor Center of St. Paul staff the pier from 1:00 to 3:00 P.M. Sundays from November through March. Wisely, no one is at the site in temperatures below 10 degrees or in the rain. Several etiquette rules have been posted as gentle reminders not to bother the wary birds. A car makes a good blind, so the "eagle-eyed" birds don't spot the spotters.

A mile south of Wabasha, turn right on State 60 and drive one and a half miles to the first gravel road to the left for the Arrowhead Bluffs Exhibit. Drivers know they're close when they spot a sign for the local golf course. Another mile and a half along the unmarked road leads to the Les Behrens farm, where a building on the grounds houses a display of stuffed musk ox, moose, deer, and other big game. The creatures peer down from every nook and cranny amid a rare collection of 220 vintage Winchester rifles dating from between 1866 and 1982. Other collectibles include hundreds of arrowheads Behrens and his family have found in their fields, plus a 12,000-year-old mammoth tusk and similar antiquities.

Behrens' son, John, a local contractor who has worked on building projects in Russia and Alaska, constructed the exhibition space in 1985. The family put up the museum to house the collection after Behrens hinted he was considering selling it. "I would have divorced him if he ever got rid of his collection," laughed Behrens' wife, Shirley. "He would have been too grouchy to live with." The museum has turned into a popular stop for vacationers. Admission is $3.25 for adults, $2.25 for students 12-18, and $1.25 for those 6-12. A season pass is available for $6.50.

Six miles to the south of Wabasha is the magical kingdom of L.A.R.K. Land, on a frontage road off US 61 via County 18. L.A.R.K. Toys, home of bristly Gip the Vietnamese Pig and dozens of intricate carvings of trolls, wizards, prancing horses, dancing dragons, and frolicking frogs, is a wonderland of sawdust and stained basswood. The ten-year-old company was the brainchild of Donn and Sarah Kreofsky, who plan on having a masterpiece carousel with dozens of hand-carved characters cavorting around the rotating platform. "He does the dreams, I do the paper trail," said Sarah.

In an exhibition area, displays of 2,500 toy boats, 500 antique pedal cars, and 6,500 Mickey Mouses (Mice?) are on tap for the facility when it is operating by 1995. The Kreofsky toy line shows up at the Smithsonian Institution's museum shop and 2,500 other stores around the country. It's double fun to tour the workshop, past snorting Gip's little pen.

Kreofsky had been a university art professor whose family operated lumberyards where he had worked in his youth. And even as he matured, Kreofsky retained his interest in toys. "Thank heavens my mother saved mine," he recalled.

A large shop attached to the woodworking shop offers tin toys from around the world. Look into the rafters and see the resident troll smiling down on browsers. In tune with the good-old-days feel to the operation, Laffy-Taffy and eyepoppers are only ten cents, with giant whirly-pops at one dollar.

The viewing platforms at Lock and Dam No. 5 between Kellogg and Minnesota City offer primo gawking posts to watch the tugs and pleasure craft plying the river. One of eleven control structures across the nine-foot-deep navigation channel between Wabasha and Rock Island, Illinois, the dam is located along the river bottom that forms the Upper Mississippi River National Wildlife and Fish Refuge. Tundra swans, canvasbacks, wood ducks, and eagles use the nearby marshes as feeding grounds. Herons, egrets, and bitterns have large rookeries in more remote areas well away from the roads, but keen birdwatchers can still spot them coming and going on commuter runs from their nesting sites. Between the boats and the birds, there's plenty to watch.

Bass Camp resort near the lock and dam has a twenty-eight-foot-long salad bar and occasional all-you-can-eat peel-and-eat shrimp for any straggling yuppie who wanders in. The best thing about Bass Camp, however, is the group of good ol' boys around the bar discussing the state of fishing affairs over their powerful, throat-clearing boilermakers. This is a flannel-shirt, baseball-cap, and blue-jean place, closed Mondays.

For the best fish eats along this stretch of the Mississippi, drop by the Hot Fish Shop in Winona, the next city down the line on US 61. Founded as a fish market in 1931 by Henry and Helen Kowalewski, the Hot Fish Shop moved to US 61 after its downtown location was bought out for a school construction. Friends helped build the place. According to family lore, they told the Kowalewskis, "It's finished, now go make some money. When you get a little bit ahead you can pay us something." The third generation, under the combined business eyes of the founders' grandson-in-law and granddaughter Joe and Nancy Goshnet, currently runs the shop, which now includes several large fish-decorated dining rooms and a lounge. The family's secret-recipe tartar and cocktail sauces can be purchased in area stores.

Upwards of 350 pounds of Canadian walleye pike are served each week. "We buy 20,000 pounds at a time," pointed out Goshnet, demonstrating that Winona folks know a good

A paddle-wheel boat in Winona

deal when it swims past. "As we've always said, 'Good food is not cheap and cheap food is not good,'" he added.

Winona, an island city, actually sits astride a giant sandbar created by the musing of the river. A multimillion-dollar levee protected the city during the horrendous summer floods of 1993, with watermarks still visible high along the murals decorating the protective dike's white walls.

Named from the Dakota word "Wenonah," meaning "firstborn daughter," the city was settled in 1851 by steamboat Captain Orrin Smith. So the historically rich community proudly shows off its riverfront genealogy. The Julius C. Wilkie steamboat museum on the waterfront houses letters written by paddle-wheel king Robert Fulton and has walls covered with boating memorabilia. The original museum was housed in a real steamboat, destroyed by fire in 1981. A new boat was designed and finished the next year, using two smokestacks, the engine, and the wheel from the first vessel.

In addition, the *Delta Queen*, one of America's last remaining working passenger steamboats, makes regular calls on Winona, keeping the riverfront a lively place. The *Jollie Ollie*, a small charter steamboat, also makes regular summer/autumn runs along the river to keep the city's heritage alive.

Winona is also home to four major stained-glass studios, providing one of the economic mainstays for the community. Visitors can stop in at the Conway Universal Studios, 503 Center Street, to watch the glaziers and artists bending to their tasks. The shop, appropriately softened by delicate window works, fills orders for churches throughout the country. Word of mouth gets the Conway Universal name around, as clergyfolk move from parish to parish.

So if fish, steamboats, and stained glass make Winona what it is, then apples have put La Crescent on the culinary map. The Apple Capital of Minnesota got its start in 1857 when the first orchards were planted, explained the lanky Bernie Buehler, owner of Leidel's Apple Orchards and president of the Minnesota apple growers federation.

In the autumn, Leidel's and other fruit stands throughout the area explode with crimson, yellow, and green apples overflowing baskets and bags. Some thirty types of apples are produced in the region, most developed for the state's short growing season: Haralson, Honeygold, Regent, and Fireside are a few of the more popular midwestern brands, along with the nationally known Red Delicious, Jonathan, and McIntosh. In total, the state's growers annually produce about 700,000 bushels of apples, with more than a quarter of that figure coming from La Crescent.

Buehler is typical of many of the "orchardists" who farm around La Crescent. His great-grandfather homesteaded nearby, with Buehler working in orchards all his life. "We are apple farmers, just like any other crop farmer. It's always a challenge," he said past his sunburn. "Each spring, there's a new beginning. And you work hard toward this time of year when it all comes to fruition," he added, waving his hand over toward basket upon basket of ripe fruit in his stand.

Brian Nelson of Old Hickory Farms is another third-generation orchard manager, whose Apple Shed outlet can be found off US 61 in La Crescent by taking Main Street to Elm Street and on to the outskirts of town. Confronted with subdivisions creeping over the hillsides toward stock planted by his grandfather two generations ago, Nelson must deal with developers aggressively pounding on his door seeking to buy land for bedroom communities serving nearby La Crosse, Wisconsin. Yet for the time being, Nelson can stack 35,000 bushels of quality apples from his orchards in his coolers, for sale in grocery stores and road stands.

"I have mixed emotions about selling land. But the town is moving this way. I have the north end, the only way expansion can come, because the bluffs are on the south and west of the city, with the river to the east," he said, looking toward "Browntown." The encroaching cluster of tannin-colored homes seemed like mushrooms following an autumn rain. "At least, we have other orchard sites further inland that we can use," he said.

His mother, Marti Nelson, ran the orchards for twenty-two years after the death of her first husband and still helps with the sorting and packing of the fall harvest. "There's nothing like the sun rising over the bluffs here," she offered. "The deer come up the valley and there's a softness to the land. It gets in the blood," Mrs. Nelson said. "But you have to do what you have to do to survive."

La Crescent's scenic Apple Blossom Drive, actually North Elm Street, is a seven-mile drive that edges through the bluff country, returning to US 61 at Dakota to the north. Lautz Orchards and Fruit Acres are among the farming optional stops. The former offers hot apple pie and a magnificent view of Lock and Dam No. 7 down below on the river. The latter offers friendly and talkative Gordon Yates, co-owner of Fruit Acres. Yates arrived in Minnesota from Yorkshire, England, in the mid-1950s. After a Royal Navy stint during World War II, he had managed orchards in Denmark, where he had met his wife. He knows every tree on his land, roaming the plots with a cordless telephone stuck in his left shirt pocket for quick communication access.

On any drive through orchard country, travelers are advised to keep their hands in their pockets. Most communities levy a $100 fine for plucking apples unasked from trees. "Imagine if everyone went through here and kept picking the stock," one farmer lamented.

So from apples to eagles, from pottery to toys, Minnesota's Mississippi River country has plenty to offer the inquisitive backcountry motorist.

In the Area

Minnesota Department of Agriculture (for apple info): 612-297-2200

Red Wing Heritage Preservation Commission (Red Wing): 612-388-6734

T.B. Sheldon Auditorium Theatre (Red Wing): 612-388-2892

St. James Hotel (Red Wing): 800-252-1875

Anderson House (Wabasha): 612-565-4524

Wabasha Chamber of Commerce (Wabasha): 612-565-4158

Arrowhead Bluffs Exhibits/Museum (Wabasha):
612-565-3829

Lake City Chamber of Commerce (Lake City):
612-345-4123

L.A.R.K. Toys (Kellogg): 507-767-3387

Winona Convention and Visitors Bureau (Winona):
507-452-2272

Conway Universal Studios (Winona): 507-452-2272

Winona Steamboat Center (Winona): 507-454-1254

Hot Fish Shop (Winona): 507-452-5002

La Crescent Chamber of Commerce (La Crescent):
507-895-2800

Leidel's Apple Stand (La Crescent): 507-895-8221

5 ~

Blue Earth-
Worthington

Getting there: From the Twin Cities, take I-35 south to I-90, turn west, and exit at US 169. Blue Earth to Worthington, 80 miles; Twin Cities to Blue Earth, 120 miles.

Highlights: *cornfields, prairie horizons, museums, lakes, packing plants, racing turkeys, and pioneer settlements.*

Welcome to The Valley. Blue Earth, Minnesota. On a Fourth of July weekend, it's time to whip off I-90 on US 169 and search for the perfect Americana Country Road.

But what's with this big green guy wearing a bizarre combination of leotards and leaves looming over the rooftops, just visible from the interstate. The sight is startling: a smirking sixty-foot fellow in size seventy-eight shoes peeking over the Wal-Mart Discount City sign. Arms akimbo, he looks toward the highway as if he owns the place.

In a way, the Green Giant does have a financial stake in this southwest Minnesota community, home to a plant that packs thousands of cases of peas and corn each season for national distribution. The Big Green Guy is the symbol of what a well-rounded diet can do for hearty eaters.

The giant (actually a statue) hangs out in a little park immediately behind the Faribault County offices of the U.S. Department of Agriculture and the Agricultural Stabilization Conservation Service—near the Dairy Queen for desserts after eating one's veggies. A tiny red barn near the walkway leading to the statue houses the Blue Earth Visitor Center during summer months. The center is closed in the winter, but Big Green is always dapper and prepared for weather's worst. The townsfolk wrap a long scarlet scarf around his neck. Although on this muggy July Fourth, he seems to be mopping his brow.

The giant debuted in 1925, bootlegged by the Blue Earth Canning Co. from a Grimm's fairy tale. In those early days, he was more of a dwarf wearing bearskins. Ninety people were needed at the company's first small plant, processing hand-picked corn delivered by wagon. By 1929, after the company was purchased by the Minnesota Valley Canning Co., peas were added to the production line. Also in that year, the green guy had eaten all his vegetables and truly became a giant, trading in the skins for leaves.

In 1950, the firm officially became Green Giant, and old GG had ho-ho-ho-ed his way into America's consciousness. In 1979, Pillsbury purchased Green Giant, and the jolly character and the Pillsbury Doughboy probably became great pals. Grand Metropolitan Inc. (which also owns Alpo dog food and Häagen-Dazs ice cream) bought out Pillsbury/Green Giant in 1988. The firm has other packing plants in south-central Minnesota: at Le Sueur, Glencoe, and Montgomery.

Tours of the Blue Earth plant used to be offered regularly but were dropped several years ago due to safety and insurance considerations, although the signage at the Green Giant statue still indicates such excursions are available.

Guests are still welcome to visit the front office, but call 507-526-2131 in advance if you wish to view tapes on pea and corn processing. JoAnn Kehr, the plant's administrative assistant, will try to accommodate visitors, depending on her seasonal workload. The best time for a stop is during the slack winter months when operations have shut down for equipment repairs. There is more breathing space during this off-time for the staff to show the videos and explain plant operations.

The processing facilities are located on 710 East 7th Street, a tree-shaded street just off US 169. Parking is available nearby. During the packing, visitors can stand outside the plant and watch the peas and corn pour off the produce trucks onto hoppers that carry the vitamins-on-the-hoof into the plant. Just don't get too close to the steady stream of traffic.

During the August/September season, you can purchase fresh sweet corn at a small stall behind the plant for the best prices in four midwestern states. You can get a "packer's dozen" of twelve to fifteen rich yellow ears for only $1.50. Pea packing is conducted earlier in the summer, generally from middle June to July. When the plant is going full blast, shifts run from 7:00 A.M. to 7:00 P.M. and from 7:00 P.M. to 7:00 A.M. Up to 400 people prepare corn for packing, with 300 needed for peas. Although the corn is husked automatically, more hand work is required to get the vegetables placed properly in the cleaning equipment. The free-spirit peas just keep rolling along in their own round green torrent.

The 8,000-pound jolly giant statue was dedicated on July 6, 1979, to commemorate the last complete I-90 link between East and West coasts. A slab of gold pavement (since removed) was installed on the city's west side to mark the occasion. What was once US 16, which had previously handled much of the transcontinental traffic, was carved up between Minnesota counties for maintenance responsibility.

It's along old County 16 that the traveler can find secret hideaways, fishing holes, pump organs, coughing steam engines, and balding good ol' boys. Faribault County is where it all starts, almost smack center in southern Minnesota where the border hugs the top of Iowa. The county, population about 20,000, was named for Jeane Baptiste Faribault, a well-known French Canadian trader. The first permanent white settler was Moses Sailor, who built his cabin where the city of Blue Earth is now. He planted potatoes and corn so his family could survive the harsh Minnesota winter, living in his covered wagon for almost a year before he got around to building a house.

Southern Minnesota was a hardscrabble place for its early settlers, who lamented their lack of money, provisions, and housing. The 1850s were tough on families who had to live in dank, dark sod houses, as well as battle drought, locusts, floods, and loneliness. But by the 1860s, some progress was made, as more of the shoulder-high grass was plowed under. Frame farmhouses popped up on the prairie like mushrooms after the rain. The weather cooperated and crops were plentiful. But in August 1862, a Dakota Sioux uprising struck deep terror into the hearts of settlers on their scattered farms. From the western frontier refugees poured into Blue Earth and other perceived havens. They carried horror stories of an attack on New Ulm, fifty miles to the north. Panic spread all the way to the Mississippi River Valley. It was estimated that more than 2,500 persons eventually fled Faribault County (almost the entire population), leaving only about 100 men behind to defend a hastily erected fortification around Blue Earth. The primitive roads all the way to Albert Lea were clogged with horse-drawn wagons, ox carts, and people on foot fleeing the Sioux. But the Native American warriors never came into the area and no clashes were reported between the cultures, although a herd of cattle on the horizon near the escape route was mistakenly thought to be a war party.

Minnesota is farm country

After a few weeks, however, most people returned to their homes when word spread that the militia had reportedly broken up the rebellion. Still shaken and nervous, the locals took to the plow again and solidified their hold on the countryside. With the Indian threat behind them, the farmers still had to contend with a more insidious problem. Unscrupulous bankers sometimes loaned money to new arrivals at 30 to 60 percent interest, causing many homesteaders and businesses to eventually collapse under the debt burden. Those who survived were subsequently wary in dealing with outsiders.

But it was hard to leave the rich fertile land, once part of an immense glacial lake. Formed by runoff from the glaciers, the mineral-rich water eventually drained into what is now the Blue Earth and Minnesota rivers. The rolling hills left behind by the departure of those enormous slow-moving ice cubes have helped Faribault County become one of the top soybean-and-corn-producing areas in Minnesota.

The term "blue earth" was used as early as 1700 when French explorer Charles le Sueur found some colored lumps of clay around today's city of Mankato (in the Sioux tongue, "mankato" means blue earth, which the tribesmen streaked on their faces). Le Sueur was sure he had discovered copper ore. Wrong! None of that valuable metal was ever found in the vicinity, although Le Sueur supposedly dangled a vision of untapped riches in front of potential investors for his expeditions.

The county highway that parallels today's interstate rises and falls over the gentle ridges around Blue Earth, rolling through Guckeen, Fairmont, and on to Worthington. The road passes small gas stations, castle-like feed elevators, ma and pa hardware stores, and acres upon acres of cropland. Marking the July Fourth weekend, U.S. flags flutter from light poles lining village streets. Farmhouses display colorful red, white, and blue bunting from their front porches. By evening, it will be sparkler time.

The Blue Earth River slides its slow, muddy way through the town of Blue Earth. The community of 4,200 was originally called Blue Earth City when surveyors laid out the streets for the town's enthusiastic founding fathers and mothers. The city has an 1890s courthouse complete with intricate masonry and stonework, Victorian homes, and a spread of comfortable parks perfect for a Fourth of July picnic. In fact, on this hot holiday, sunburned farmer Dale Russell, his wife Francine, and their nine-year-old son, Brian, pull up for some sodas at the 7th and Main Kwik-Stop. Max, their one-year-old St. Bernard, lolls over the back panel of their pickup. Fireworks are on the agenda for the night's activities.

Ralph and Denise Carlson roar into the service station parking lot on their Harley cycles, leather fringe flying and red bandanna headgear in place. They are returning from the

Freedom Rally in Humboldt, Iowa, an annual summertime biker confab. "Independence Day. Yep, freedom in America is the chance to do what you want to do. Like an open-air bike ride cross-country," Carlson says, wiping the road grime from his forehead.

At his storefront shop on Main Street, just up the road from the Green Giant plant and adjacent to Dancers Unlimited (for stretch aerobics), youthful Paul Amundson peruses his collection of refurbished player pianos. With impresario elegance, he cranks up a couple of music boxes, and their tinny, clickety-clack sounds echo out on the broad, quiet avenue. Amundson started selling the pianos and "one-man-band" instruments when he was only twenty. Seven years later, he has the corner on the nickelodeon market throughout a 1,200-mile radius of his home in nearby Frost, six miles southeast of Blue Earth.

Amundson patches leather, lays in new keyboards, and generally spruces up tired, battered old machines that have seen rowdier days in billiard parlors, saloons, and honky-tonks from Deadwood to Des Moines. In a cool basement workshop, after hanging a "Be Right Back" sign on his front door, Amundson shows his ongoing work on several used pianos, a coinola, and assorted piles of other somethings-or-another. It takes about two months to nurse instruments back to health, to where "The Entrance of the Gladiators" bellows as it should. Prices start at $2,700 for a fully renovated machine (they can be rented!).

An entrepreneur who sees opportunity everywhere, Amundson gives Model T rides in the summer to visitors who come knocking with $5 in their hands. He puts the "closed" sign back in his window, salutes his forty-eight-star U.S. flag, and cranks up the jalopy to rack and roll around the courthouse square. He rumbles past the best of the old homes along 2nd and Moore streets and points out other sights near downtown. Call Amundson at 507-526-7285 to check on which pipe organ is primed for action . . . or to have his old car curbside and ready to roll.

"We do a booming business during Green Giant Days. Those are usually the last weekend in June," he confides, dropping a coin into a player machine that blasts out some wonderful Fourth of July rouser on the artfully enclosed drum, triangle, piano, and xylophone.

As you depart Blue Earth westward on County 16, the road follows a rail bed for a time and then cuts across the flat corn country. Just before leaving town, near US 169 where the Blue Earth River slices through this edge of town, you'll see a canoe landing that seems perfect for setting out on lazy July driftings.

The Iowa, Minnesota, and Northwestern Railroad brought "civilization" to the Minnesota frontier in 1900. Its tracks clawed across the farmland, linking villages that would grow into towns and bypassing others, which led eventually to their slow deaths. The rail line extended the six miles from Blue Earth to Derby, which changed its name to Guckeen to honor the farmer who sold land on which to build a depot. In the first decade of the century, Guckeen boasted of a bank, a blacksmith shop, and a main street lined with businesses. When you drive through the town today, it is obvious that even a railroad can't save some communities. Scraps of paper drift across the highway to lodge in the doorways of shuttered shops. The hometown school is boarded up, with graffiti lending a Picasso-ish feel to the weatherbeaten facade. Only the four white silos at the Farmer's Elevator and several metal storage sheds stand as monuments to the rural backbone that keeps the few residents remaining in town.

Another two miles west on 16 is the Faribault-Martin county line. County 16 becomes County 26. For another ten miles to Fairmont, the road is straight as an arrow across the landscape. You will pass Lake Imogene and its campground on the south side of the highway, a pleasant picnic place perfect for a July getaway.

Fairmont, the City of Lakes, was first called Fair Mount because of its vista overlooking Lake Sisseton. Eighteen other bass-filled glacier lakes dot the area, keeping up the image of the city as a fisherfolk paradise. Five of the lakes are interconnected within the city limits, so no kid has an excuse that a swimming beach is too far out of the way. This land wasn't always such a delight, with the first settlers living on frozen turnips as four feet of winter snow piled up on the prairie in 1856. Most of the first settlers packed it in after only a few years of arguing with Ma Nature. The Sioux uprising of 1862 also sent many settlers stampeding eastward. Soldiers on the way to battle the tribes found horses in stables and food on tables, testimony to a hurried getaway by the whites.

In 1873, a colony of English gentlemen farmers and their families attempted to make a go of it near Fairmont. But locusts destroyed the colony's first bean crop in less than a day, causing many of the folks to head back to the perceived safer climes of Great Britain. A few hung on, however, eventually forming a sporting club that hunted foxes and played soccer.

At Zanke's Sporting Goods, 445 Lake Avenue, no one talks about riding to the hounds. You can't miss the place. A sign out front roars "LIVE BAIT," backed by nearby Lake Sisseton's outdoorsy aroma of reeds and summer-warm water. Zanke's is a guys' "boat and hook 'em" place, where baseball caps line the ceiling beams with unmentionable quotations and the chat is all about walleyes. Burly, bearded Jim Zanke, owner of the shop since the early 1980s, wears a Schlitz Beer cap shoved back on his head. Budd and Hall lakes south of town on County 15 are the quality spots for dropping in a line and a lure, he reports. In response to a question as to what's best to fish for, Zanke says with simple fisherman's logic, "Whatever is biting."

He adds that his minnows are guaranteed to catch fish or die trying. Mike Taggert and other fishermen in the crowded store—exploding as it is with lures, leeches, and lines—guffaw at the old joke. Their idea of the perfect Fourth of July is . . . fishing. Of course.

Just as it should in any small American town, the city band still performs every Tuesday evening during June and the first week in July. Concerts take place in the park at 4th Street and Lake Avenue. Blankets, lawn chairs, and bug repellent are the only necessities. The Fairmont Martins amateur baseball team battles its hardball opponents at 7:30 P.M. each Sunday and Wednesday night throughout the summer on the high school field. If all that isn't enough to keep Fairmontians busy, every Friday from early June through mid-August, the city hosts a Friday in the Park program that ranges from the Vikings' football team cheerleaders to karate demonstrations. Shows begin at 12:15 P.M. in the Downtown Plaza.

Skipping a season ahead, Fairmont literally glows around the Christmas holidays, a factor to consider in mid-July when the sun pops the corn on the stalks. Ward Park on Lake Sisseton has a fascinating display of lighting that does wonders for chasing away the wintertime blues. More than 30,000 bulbs decorate iron frames depicting fountains, deer, bears, and geese. Lincoln Park on the eastern shore of George Lake has a Christmas theme, as well. Livingston Cabin, an original settler's home in the park, is decorated with garlands and evergreens with turn-of-the-century gifts placed beneath the boughs. Displays in both parks are turned on the Friday after Thanksgiving, lighted daily from 5:00 P.M. to 11:00 P.M. through January 2.

Heritage Acres Agriculture Interpretive Center is located on the old Reuben Ward homestead on Fairmont's northwest side as County 26 heads into the sunset. The living-history center offers more than just a window peek at the past with its schoolhouse, church, homestead, and other frontier buildings to peruse. It conducts year-round activities demonstrating pioneer life on the prairies. In April, curators plant oats using horse-drawn equipment. In May, there are corn plantings and a wedding. June has Dairy Days, followed by July's cutting and shocking of the oat crop. Each Fourth of July, a Bluegrass Festival is held on the site, with top regional bands performing from 1:00 P.M. to 6:00 P.M. A threshing bee is held in August, an arts and crafts fair in September, and a corn harvest in October. For specific dates, call 507-235-5547 or 507-235-3535. The Heritage Center is open from 10:00 A.M. to 5:00 P.M. Monday through Friday, with tours available by appointment. Admission is $3.

The nearby National Guard Armory hosts a regular Saturday and Sunday flea market, where the careful buyer can find anything from collectibles to what-the-heck-is-that. Leaving town, you'll find an American sampler of Fourth of July music on KCHE-FM, aired from Mankato State University. The swelling music from Copland and other great American composers is a fitting backdrop to a country road drive.

And there it is. Welcome to Welcome. The village of 855, six miles west of Fairmont, was named after an early resident who must have been the friendly sort. The community is a rail hub, with a maze of interlocking tracks adjacent to the standard Minnesota monument to a way of life—the grain elevator. The Chicago and Northwestern Railroad has a straight link from South Dakota through Welcome, where it meets the Chicago, St. Paul, and Pacific Line. Timothy's Irish Pub is hunkered down on Welcome's west end, on the north side of County 26 where it intersects with Dugan Street. Drop in for a tip of the pint, or something more mellow for anyone driving.

The Fox Lake Game Refuge, where State 4 cuts south across County 26, is a warren of marshes and swampland ringing several lakes near Sherburn. In 1863, the last free-ranging buffalo in southwestern Minnesota was shot near Fox Lake by a soldier patrolling for angry Sioux. That wasn't the only notable death in the area. The first murder in Martin County was recorded near Fox Lake in the 1870s when a storekeeper from Yankton, South Dakota, was found shot to death while on his way to buy supplies in Mankato. No one was ever convicted of the crime, but "Dead Man's Slough" was the moniker forever applied to the swamp where the body was found.

Jackson snuggles between the east and west branches of the Des Moines River. In the 1850s, roving bands of Indians killed a number of settlers in Spirit Lake, Iowa, just eight miles south of the town. That, coupled with the Sioux Uprising in 1862, meant there were a lot of nervous settlers. Nine area homesteaders were killed during the Sioux rebellion, and the survivors—the entire population of the county—fled. Troops reported that in over a year of patrolling they never spotted a civilian.

Things are much quieter now in Jackson, although there was plenty of excitement in 1979, 1980, 1984, and 1986 when the girls at the high school won the state Class A gymnastic championships. There's also plenty of dining action at Charlie the Greek's Food and Cocktails, a local hot spot at Sherman and 3rd streets.

Take County 14 west from Jackson, past the pastures packed with polled Herefords and fields of soybeans growing through their July adolescence. The mailbox on the Dale Shubert farm about four miles along the road is mounted on a toy tractor. Cross under I-90, turn left at Jackson County 12, and continue cruising west. Roll up the sleeves, adjust the dark glasses, hang the left arm out the driver's side window, crank up Bruce Springsteen's "Born in the USA" and revel in the bright sun. You'll whiz through unincorporated Rost and continue on to County 1, the border with Nobles County. Turn south on County 1, cross I-90 again, and pick up County 35 into Worthington.

This city, the Nobles County seat, was the brainchild of the National Colony Company. This temperance group figured that windswept southern Minnesota would be a great place in which to settle and raise families, far from the influence of the big, bad urban environment. In 1871, their first houses went up. Unfortunately, in 1873, grasshoppers came to dinner . . . uninvited and hungry. It was enough to make even the temperance types turn to drink as the swarms devoured everything green in sight. The insects savored the menu around Worthington so much they returned each summer for five years. Farms failed and homesteaders resorted to selling muskrat pelts to survive the harsh winters.

Today, the grasshoppers have long been gone. Descendants of the surviving muskrats snuffle around the sloughs. And farming has gone to the birds.

Raising turkeys has become one of the prime industries in Nobles County. The birds provide a relatively quick financial return, even if they sound like a room of mothers-in-law at a poker party. In the 1930s when the industry was launched, many of the gobblers were processed at a plant operated by E. O. Olson, an inveterate traveler. In 1938, Olson visited Cuero, Texas, another major turkey center—one that held a Turkey Festival every year.

When Olson came back to Worthington to report on the fun he had had, the hometown folks loved the idea of having their own turkey party with all the trimmings: parade, dinner, dance, and kids' activities. Subsequently, King Turkey Day was launched. Gaining national recognition over the years, the festivities have become de rigueur for politicians and entertainers. Since then, the program has grown to include a parade of turkeys . . . and appearances by such politicians as Lyndon B. Johnson, Nelson Rockefeller, Rev. Jesse Jackson,

Robert Kennedy, Hubert Humphrey, and Richard Nixon. You can imagine the curbside jokes that follow the trotting turks and talking pols.

Since 1973, Cuero and Worthington have competed in the Great Gobbler Gallop, in which community leaders from both towns race their fastest birds down the main street of the opposing community. One heat is held in each town, with the winner of both earning the walnut-and-gold Traveling Turkey Trophy of Tumultuous Triumph. The loser doesn't wind up in the oven but goes home with the Circulating Consolation Cup of Consummate Commiseration.

At the Minnesota race, up to 30,000 spectators urge on the likes of Ruby Begonia (the Pride of Texas) or Worthington's Paycheck (so called because the bird's handler says it goes so fast). The Worthington run is held the second weekend following Labor Day, with the Texas race held on the first weekend in October. The event is held even in "fowl" weather.

But a Minnesota warning. If you spot a flashing red light in your rearview mirror, followed by sirens and a police officer urging you to pull over, don't panic. Each year, an unsuspecting motorist on I-90 is invited to be the city's guest for a turkey dinner during the festival. The driver will also appear in the King Turkey Day Parade. That's enough reason to travel the backcountry roads.

Even without the turkeys, the Worthington area has a full plate of travel side dishes. The Nobles County Pioneer Village, south of I-90 between exits 43 and 45 and west of the Nobles County Fairgrounds, is a complete pioneer village. But after a rain, be careful on the muddy road leading into the fairground parking lot. Ruts and puddles do wonders for an auto's undergear. A paving job is promised for the future.

The Pioneer Village is a real kid place, where lessons about living in the "good old days" are subtly taught with hands-on fun. In mid-July each year, the village hosts a free Kid Fest sponsored by the Worthington Optimist Club. A doll

71

A future Traveling Turkey of Tumultuous Triumph

and teddy bear clinic at the festival attracts dozens of young-sters who need their damaged toys repaired. On Halloween, a pumpkin trail meanders through the village. Kids go from shop to home to store to collect candy from costumed inter-preters. Only candles are used for illumination, providing all the appropriate (but safe) thrills and chills of tiptoeing through an old-fashioned evening.

A display of metal-wheeled lawnmowers, with a sign indicating that guests are welcome to mow the grass, stands just inside the main entrance. Plenty of kids give it a try. The resulting swaths are uneven, but the labor is free, so the idea makes a lot of sense.

Pioneer Village director Roy Reimer is clad in bib over-alls, bending over a red 1915 Galloway nine-horsepower gas engine in an attempt to get it running. "All thirty-five buildings have been collected from around the county. The general store was once a saloon, so we did make some modi-fications. But mostly, this is how Worthington would have looked in the 1880s," he says. A boardwalk along the main street passes the *Western Advance* newspaper office and adja-cent shops, including one that was used by traveling sales-men to showcase their wares. In front of a nearby house, a woman demonstrates washing clothes in a tub of boiling water, à la frontier.

Al Swanson, Pioneer Village president, proudly points out that the Village's ancient Bigelow grain elevator was going to be razed several years ago. As die-hard collectors, the historical society jumped at the opportunity and rescued the metal building from the wrecking ball and cutting torch. "All the kids turned out to watch us move the structure and put it back up," he recalls.

Admission for adults is $3, with kids pegged at 50 cents. From May through September, the complex is open from 1:00 to 5:00 P.M. Monday through Saturday and from 9:00 A.M. to 5:00 P.M. on Sunday.

By now, the sun is ready to slide into the Dakotas. Youngsters are collecting at parks and ball fields, eager for holiday fireworks. Firecrackers poppity-pop in the fading light. It's been another great Fourth of July.

In the Area

Green Giant Canning Company (Blue Earth): 507-526-2131

Paul Amundson Enterprise/Player Pianos (Blue Earth): 507-526-7285

Zanke Sporting Goods (Fairmont): 507-235-6931

Fairmont Area Chamber of Commerce (Fairmont): 507-235-5547

Worthington Area Convention & Visitors Bureau (Worthington): 507-372-2919

Nobles County Historical Society Pioneer Village (Worthington): 507-376-3125 or 507-376-4431

6 ~

Luverne-
Pipestone

Getting there: From the Twin Cities, take US 12 west to State 23 south to Pipestone; from Iowa, drive north on US 75 to Pipestone; from South Dakota, take I-90 east to Beaver Creek and drive north on State 23, or go to Luverne and drive north on US 75.

Highlights: *buffalo herds, ancient quarries at Pipestone National Monument, Song of Hiawatha pageant, band festivals, summertime baseball, Civil War reenactment, and repertory theater.*

Earth was bountiful and we were all surrounded with blessings of the Great Mystery.

—Luthern Standing Bear

The wind is a constant hymn in Blue Mounds State Park, blowing in from the vast, flat plains. Southwestern Minnesota stirs in the breeze; the grasses wave and treetops shimmer as the hot air moves over the rough landscape. Here on Eagle Rock, high above the surrounding flatlands at 1,730 feet above sea level, a keen eye can see Iowa to the south and South Dakota to the west. A turgid, flood-swollen Rock River spreads across farm fields far below the hill. This is a country where the hard blue sky has sharp horizon edges.

Eagle Rock was a traditional landmark for migrating Indian tribes, as well as for pioneers trudging their slow way westward toward hoped-for riches. The monster hunk of glacier-deposited granite is 300 feet higher than the city of Luverne, whose water tower is Lilliputian-like four miles away to the south. The 1,500-acre state park is six miles north of I-90, that concrete slash slicing across the upper plains on a mad rush to the Rocky Mountains. Sixteen miles north lies the red granite city of Pipestone.

Thirteen miles of easily hiked trails loop over the ridge line, edging outward high above the park's visitor's center. The building, cut deep into the hill, is west on County 8 about a mile off US 75, while the main entrance to the park is further north on US 75 off County 20. The park itself has seventy-three campsites, forty-three sites with electrical hookups, a primitive camp for groups, picnic grounds, a swimming beach, and, the most fun, a bison herd. The ponderous critters can be seen from raised platforms overlooking their winter and summer grazing ranges. Naturally, one should not—repeat not—pet the bison. There is a $4 day-fee at the park, but the interpretive center is free.

From 1960 to 1975, the center structure was the home of award-winning regional writer Frederick Manfred. His richly woven tales of Native American and pioneer life have thrilled readers of several generations.

Atop the park building is a tower, which Manfred called his "tipi." From there, he could ponder and write. By climbing a spiral wrought-iron staircase, today's park guests can gaze out on the inspiring vista. Many of Manfred's books, such as *Wanderlust* and the Scarlet Plume series, line the shelves in this circular upper room.

His novels nestle next to works by John Steinbeck and well-used copies of *National Geographic* magazine. The interpretive center is still looking for book donations of all types to round out its collection for a library it is establishing there.

The state site is one of the largest prairie parks in Minnesota, perched on an outcrop of stone called Sioux Quartzite. The hard, purplish-red stone was prized by settlers, who fashioned courthouses, store fronts, and schools from its massive strength. Pockets of the richly colored, billion-year-old rock have been carved out from the hillsides, where laborers toiled under the broiling sun a century ago. Their chisel and blast marks can still be easily seen on the exposed cliffs throughout the park. Because of the amount of this stone used in the public buildings, the towns in this corner of Minnesota are unlikely to blow away.

An interesting archaeological feature in the park has also withstood the ravages of rain, snow, and wind. At Blue Mounds' southern perimeter is a 1,250-foot-long line of rocks aligned in a straight east-west direction. No one knows who built it or why. Yet on the first day of spring and autumn, the sunrise and sunset are perfectly lined up along the tumble of boulders and smaller stones. The "structure" is hidden amid the bushes and flowering plants along Burr Oak Trail leading out from the interpretive center.

The park's highest hill is an eye-closing place where a visitor can loll against the sun-warmed Eagle Rock and its jumble of cousins tumbled nearby. Feel the breeze and sense the rustle of bearded wheat grass. This is a gentle place, punctuated by the cries of cheerful meadowlarks whose musical dueling echoes from left and right. The outcroppings of stone terminate in a mile-and-a-half-long cliff that rises a sheer ninety feet above the prairie floor. Red clover, prairie rose, milkweed, and alumroot add their rainbow colors to the landscape. The observant hiker can even find prickly pear cacti in Blue Mounds State Park, one of the few places in Minnesota where it grows. Explosions of yellow dot the shallow earth in late June and early July when the cacti flower.

The rock hummocks and thin soil protected this land from the onslaught of plows that devoured the more fertile ground around what is now the park. Transplanting and seeding of native plants is helping bring back the original prairie look damaged by grazing from domestic animals. Even fire is used to control the exotic foreign plants and stimulate growth of the native species.

Edging away from the giant rock, stroll along the 0.8-mile Lower Mounds Trail or the 0.4-mile Upper Mounds Trail. Both eventually link for another 0.8-mile hike above the buffaloes' summer pasture. From this height, lumpy brown animal shapes dot the grassland below. Up here, the wind carries spirit songs, taken by author Manfred and made integral to his tales of warriors and their families who once roamed these hills. Their chants rise from the ground as does steam from the heated earth after an early summer's downpour.

> *Come buffalo, come.*
> *Pa-Pa, Ho-He!*
> *We wish to eat you.*
> *Give us your strength.*
> *Ho-He! We thank you.*

The Native Americans used everything from the buffalo, from the brains to bones. Even the skin on the hind leg was naturally shaped for moccasins.

> *Out of the earth I sing for them,*
> *The animals, I sing for them.*

When you leave the park, passing a herd of grazing black-and-white Holstein dairy cows in a muddy feeding lot, the rush of contemporary life strikes home. Trucks roar past, chasing away the Sioux prairie songs. A trio of young bicyclists at the intersection of US 75 and 20 pauses before darting across the roadway. They pedal furiously over the concrete and on toward their farm home on the horizon.

The kids probably go to school in Luverne, site of an annual Tri-State Band festival held the last Saturday of September. The festival highlights parade and field competition for high schools from Minnesota, Iowa, Nebraska, South Dakota, and Canada—actually making it more than a three-state affair. To be sure everyone has a great seat, the parade competition is held in the morning along Main Street, with plenty of drums, bugles, and flash. Field competition starts in the early afternoon at the Luverne high school athletic field.

Visitors to Luverne don't mind being buffaloed when they drop by the town the first weekend in June. It's part of the fun at Buffalo Days. A parade just for kids kicks off in the early morning Saturday, followed immediately by another parade with floats and area bands. An auto show, horseshoe pitching competition, BMX races, softball tournament, and an arts and crafts fair keep the crowds moving through the community. A buffalo-chip-throwing competition is held in the city park along the banks of the Rock River. Sunday's activities include a fly-in breakfast at the airport, where everyone is welcome, even if they don't swoop in on a 747. An open house at Blue Mounds State Park follows, with tasty (honest!) buffalo burgers for sale. Interpreters give tours of the park, with discussions about the resident buffaloes.

Between band programs and buffaloes, it's a wonder that Luvernites have time for other activities. They seem to be running all the time, especially during the Border to Border Triathlon that starts during the second week of August in Luverne and ends at Crane Lake, on the Minnesota-Canada border. Crane Lake is near the wilds of the Boundary Waters Canoe Area Wilderness (BWCAW) in far northeastern Minnesota. An international field of competitors, with a minimum of sixty two-person teams, starts off with (what else in Luverne?) a weekend parade down Main Street. The triathlon begins the next day at 6:00 A.M. with a 200-mile bike race into central Minnesota. On the second day, teams bike another 200 miles into northeastern Minnesota. On the third day, participants alternate on a fifty-mile run, concluding with a fifty-mile canoe race that ends at the border.

For a more casual activity, there's the Blue Mound Opry at the city's restored Historic Palace Theater. Charlie and Kati Walhof are the personable hosts for this program of country-western and old-time music, as well as funny vaudeville routines. Seats are only $6, with shows offered at 6:00 and 8:00 P.M. the last Tuesday of each month from April through December. Upstairs in the theater is a museum with old posters and memorabilia of the heyday of the traveling road show.

A must-tour in Luverne is the Hinkly House Museum, a massive quartzite Queen Anne home built in 1892 by R. B. Hinkly, a local quarry owner who made out really well during western Minnesota's explosive frontier growth. While his kids had plenty of fun growing up there, jumping up and down on the surrounding stone walls and riding the backs of massive stone lions guarding the front porch, they never really had a blast. Luckily. You see, dad used to store his dynamite in the basement, in a storage area reached by a brick-lined tunnel. Hinkly usually kept the fuses and caps for his blasting operations in an upstairs library closet.

Aside from such tempting of fate, Hinkly was a fairly regular guy. His family traced its roots back to the Plymouth Colony in Massachusetts, and an ancestor signed the Declaration of Independence. After the turn of the century, Hinkly bought up vast tracts of land in the Rio Grande Valley, where he introduced large-scale irrigation, which helped establish the citrus industry.

To get a better look at the stone quarries from which Luverne and surrounding communities took their building

materials, drive west ten miles from Luverne on I-90 to
State 23. Turn north and drive seventeen miles to Jasper and
the Quarry Visitors Center. Photos and other displays in the
restored downtown building depict contemporary and old-
time quarry processes. The city celebrates its heritage with an
annual Quarry Festival in July, a KC's slow-pitch softball tournament, also in July, and the Jasper Community "Blowhards"
band concert in August. The Jasper Quarry Festival, held the
third weekend in July, offers fire truck rides, an antique tractor pull, a street dance, go-cart races, and bingo.

If you park on the corner of Wall and South Main streets,
you can see several historic buildings on an easy stroll. The
Jasper Historical Museum is now located in the massive Poorbaugh Building, 102 East Wall Street. The structure was built,
of course, with quartzite, because the Poorbaugh Company
operated one of the three quarries near the city. To peek inside
the museum for a tour, ask one of the neighboring shopkeep-
ers who has keys. The tiny frame Christianson House was the
community's first store, built in 1888 and refurbished in 1976.

An active quarry encompassing about 100 acres is still in
operation on the southwest side of the village. A viewing area
allows visitors to watch how the stone is now sheared away
from the cliff edge by means of a special wire device. In
the old days, labor-intensive hand work was involved. A
video describing the quarrying system is also available at the
museum.

Four miles north of Jasper on State 23 is Split Rock Creek
State Park, near Ihlen. Camping, boating, and fishing are
available, with the Archway Bridge and Dam providing the
best photo opportunities. The structure was built of native
quartzite in the mid-1930s.

Another seven miles north of Jasper on State 23 is
the Pipestone National Monument, where history, geology,
and people come together in a definitely spirit way. Native

Native Americans chip out the soft stone at Pipestone Monument to shape into pipes and animal totems

Americans began quarrying at this site as early as the seventeenth century. Carvers prized the relatively soft stone for pipes and sacred objects. What is now the site of the monument was a neutral ground where many nations could work together in peace, each with its own quarry area. In 1858, the Yankton Sioux secured free and unrestricted access to the area, but sold their claim to the federal government, a fact that still angers some younger contemporary Native Americans. The national monument was signed into existence in 1937 and then opened to the public, with limited quarrying of the soft red stone allowed only to Indians with a permit. Tribes working the site have included Eskimo, Cheyenne, Comanche, Chippewa, Sioux, and numerous others. Only hammers and chisels are allowed as tools in the ancient pits, some of which have been used by the same families for generations.

Each year, between 14,000 and 15,000 guests visit the national monument, located on the north side of the city of Pipestone. Take Hiawatha Avenue from downtown to North 9th Street and turn left just past the Song of Hiawatha pageant grounds. The center is open from Memorial Day to Labor Day from 8:00 A.M. to 6:00 P.M. Monday through Friday and from 8:00 A.M. to 8:00 P.M. Saturday and Sunday. Winter weekday hours are from 8:00 A.M. to 5:00 P.M. Seniors, Native Americans, and youngsters sixteen and under are free. Otherwise admission is $2, or $4 per family.

Surrounding the main interpretive center is an explosion of color: daisy, wild plum, and yellow goatbeard present their rainbow hues. An oriole trills from a signboard that tells guests that they are entering sacred ground. Inside the building are booths where Native Americans make and sell stone pipes, animal totems, and other objects. Cynthia Crow Brady, a Sisseton Sioux, makes turtles. "They represent long life and are a symbol of fertility," she explains, shaping and polishing a tiny figurine.

Jim Cochran, manager of the Pipestone Indian Shrine Association, which operates a gift shop at the center, traces his heritage to several tribes. "What we do here as a craftworker is a matter of personal interpretation. Yet we are keeping tradition alive," he explains. "The people who come here to quarry still perform a ceremony, but it is very private, done whenever tourists aren't around. Our spirituality comes from the heart and is as diverse as we are individuals," he says.

Cochran indicates that some Native Americans object to the sale of the polished stone artifacts to non-Indians, but he counters by saying that the items take on their special significance when blessed by a medicine man. Until then, he suggests, they could be used to help share the profound symbolism inherent in Indian culture. Behind Cochran is a wall lined with handmade pipes. Each has a card indicating the Native American artist who made the piece. Spirit-wise, it is important to walk the Circle Trail, a path that wends around the rear of the monument. The hike is needed to absorb the full impact of the site. The mile-long stroll takes about forty-five quiet minutes. Markers indicate the historical or geological importance of stops along the way. Rangers warn visitors to stay on the trail and out of the pits, because the loose rock causes hazardous footing.

A tract of virgin upland seen on the walking tour is typical of the prairie that existed in the Pipestone area before the settlers arrived. Standing amid the waist-high grasses, you can easily turn your mind back and imagine when the whispering wind and the birds ruled this land. As Sioux pipemaker Bill Erickson suggests as visitors walk past his craft area on their way outside, "Take nothing but pictures. Leave nothing but tracks."

Pipestone itself is an apple-pie-and-mom town where the Pipestone A's farm team plays Fourth of July hardball games, followed by ooh-and-aah fireworks at the local park. The Pipestone County Courthouse is appropriately midwestern, complete with a Grand Army of the Republic monument honoring Civil War veterans, a World War II tank (barrel plugged), and a grassy, oak-shaded lawn perfect for picnics.

A cloak-clad soldier has been on guard atop his pedestal in front of the massive dark-maroon courthouse since the statue was dedicated, with appropriate pomp and ceremony, on July 4, 1901. A World War II tank (serial number GAD 250880), entry ports welded shut, aims its cannon along the alley toward downtown. A few ragged clouds drift overhead, carried along by the breeze that ruffles the maples and oaks in the square. The soldier's stone eyes gaze across the street to where Bernice (Boots) Theel lives in a 100-year-old home at Southwest 2nd Avenue and Southwest 3rd Street.

Theel has lived for thirteen years across the street and has never minded the tank aimed at her house. "After all, I lived and worked in California before moving back here to retire," she smiles. While she celebrated the Fourth by playing cards and going out to the ball game with LaMoyne Godbey, a retired meat cutter from South Dakota, the soldier just stood there. A long list of the dead rolls up under his feet: Holms, Johnson, Kelly, Lord, Williams. The call to honor includes Spanish American War veterans. There is even a Civil War reenactment group in Pipestone, ready for at least a parade, if not for defense.

Don't just perch in a hotel room on a Wednesday or Saturday night. The local baseball team, the A's, just might be battling archrivals Renner Monarchs in a seven-inning duel. The field is straight west down Main Street, about a mile from downtown. This makes a pleasant walk on a summer evening, especially when the brilliant orange full moon creeps up over the treeline. Bashful at first, that moon can be brighter than the Fourth of July fireworks, sponsored each Independence Day by the American Legion Post No. 6.

Mick Myers, director of the Pipestone Area Chamber of Commerce, is always ready to describe the city's wonders over coffee and breakfast rolls in the Calumet Inn dining room. He rattles off a calendar of events that have made Pipestone THE tourist and arts mecca on Minnesota's western rim: the downtown has an official historical district packed with refurbished old buildings; a performing-arts center downtown boasts a year-round resident company in its own 300-seat theater; the Water Tower Park festival in late June brings artists and craftworkers from around the Upper Midwest; a Civil War encampment is held annually in August; the Song of Hiawatha pageant, listed as one of the state's top twenty-five attractions, draws international visitors throughout the summer to watch the pageant that has been staged by town residents since the early 1950s; the Festival of Trees and the Christmas on the Prairie pageant put sparkle into the year's end.

In keeping with Pipestone's heartland theme, Myers points out that Aaron Copland's *The Tender Land* was presented in Les and Lany Kallsen's farmyard in the summer of 1993. Performed by the University of Minnesota's opera theater, the sold-out show depicted life on a midwestern farm in the 1930s. Kallsen's cows downwind in the background provided some authentic sound effects.

Before you head out of Pipestone, a stop at Lange's Cafe at the junction of State 23 and US 75 is in order, especially for a hot ham dinner ($4.75) and eight-inch-high German chocolate cake (if you have to ask the cost, you don't deserve a piece). Opposite the Chamber of Commerce, Lange's is open twenty-four hours a day, seven days a week. It's a place where bald guys named Curley talk storm clouds, Minnesota Twins, and pork bellies with retired farmers (all named Bill) in corner booths over steaming black coffee. They hitch wide, fire-engine-red suspenders high over broad stomachs tackled by gravity, push feed caps back from sunburned brows, and expostulate about life on the prairie.

Lange's, "Where Old Friends Meet" as the sign out front says, was opened by Spyron and Edith Chaney in 1931. The cafe was purchased in 1956 by Sid and Roy Lange. Nephew Steve runs it now. Grain truckers call it home, as do seniors and the ladies' auxiliary of this or that. True to its small-town, kick-back nature, the cafe is a happy blend of folks and eating habits. Harvester Perfecto cigars and KitKat candy bars battle for space near the cash register. A pie display rack groans under the weight of calories.

Pipestone is hard to forget, even when driving away. The last sight of the town is visible for miles above the expanse of rich farmland. The tank atop its 132-foot water tower is shaped like an Indian pipe bowl. Then, almost as suddenly as it appeared, Pipestone is lost to the rolling prairie.

In the Area

Blue Mounds State Park: 507-283-4892 (Park Office);
507-283-4548 (Visitor Center)

Blue Mound Opry (Luverne): 507-283-4588

Luverne Chamber of Commerce, Historic Palace Theatre
Building: 507-283-4061

Jasper Development Corporation (Jasper): 507-345-3050

Pipestone Convention & Visitors Bureau (Pipestone):
507-825-3316

Pipestone Indian Shrine Association (Pipestone):
507-825-5463

The Song of Hiawatha (Pipestone): 507-825-4126 or 825-3316

7 ~

White Earth Reservation

Getting there: From the Twin Cities, take I-94 to US 59, then north to County 13 or State 20; or take US 10 to US 59. From North Dakota, take US 10 to State 32, then turn east on State 113 or State 200; or take 10 to 59 north for a more leisurely drive.

Highlights: *wild rice harvesting; bass fishing; wilderness and resort camping; scenic attractions; acres of forestland; Lake Itasca, birthplace of the Mississippi River; Shooting Star Casino; frontier museums.*

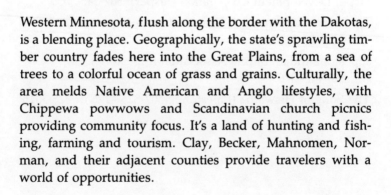

Western Minnesota, flush along the border with the Dakotas, is a blending place. Geographically, the state's sprawling timber country fades here into the Great Plains, from a sea of trees to a colorful ocean of grass and grains. Culturally, the area melds Native American and Anglo lifestyles, with Chippewa powwows and Scandinavian church picnics providing community focus. It's a land of hunting and fishing, farming and tourism. Clay, Becker, Mahnomen, Norman, and their adjacent counties provide travelers with a world of opportunities.

The neon glitz of the multimillion-dollar Shooting Star gambling casino at Mahnomen, with its parking lot packed with out-of-state motor coaches, is barely a forty-five minute drive from the quiet, pine-shaded headwaters of the Mississippi River. There, at Lake Itasca State Park, a half-million visitors a year wade across the rocky-bottomed stream that marks the birthplace of America's mightiest waterway.

There's a rhythm of Chippewa life on the White Earth Indian Reservation. It spins with the seasons, where Mother Earth asserts her strength. Power is evident in the dew-splashed late August dawns, where spiderwebs sparkle in the chokecherry bushes and mist softens the tamarack swamps.

Here, the heart is put at ease.

As the sun crawls above the pine tops, the night withdraws and the yawning day stretches skyward. A crow caw-caws in the pink distance of morning sky, the bird's harsh hello contrasting with the lament of evening's loons.

A soft swishing of reeds rises above the backwater stillness as canoes are launched through clumps of cattails. It's wild rice harvest time on the reservation. Seeking stands of the plump nutty "caviar" of grains that in some places tower ten to twelve feet high, the small boats edge around dozens of lakes. The stands are especially good in the Tamarac Wildlife Refuge in the center of the reservation, about 200 miles northwest of the Twin Cities.

Dorothy and Darwin Stevens are almost hidden by tall rushes near a weedy landing. Life partners, they smile at each other.

"Come, Old Man, it's ricing time," says Dorothy, perching in the bow of the canoe. Darwin just smiles at the loving jibe and pulls his wide-brimmed hat lower toward the laugh crinkles around his eyes. Using a long pole, Dawin pushes his way along, the canoe barely making a sound. Hungry fish roil to the surface with a flip of a fin and swiftly disappear.

Harvesting wild rice

In a second canoe, Denny St. Clair spots a heavy cluster of rice, its thick dark ears bowing three feet above the placid lake surface. Putting down his push pole, St. Clair picks up his "knockers." The two cedar sticks are the traditional means used by his tribe to sweep ripe rice from its stalks into the bottom of the canoe. St. Clair doesn't mind working alone. He has harvested for more than forty years and knows the best ricing locales a hundred miles around.

The stroke is steady. Twack, twack, twack. One of his knocker sticks bends the rice over the canoe, the other swiftly sweeps the ready heads into the boat. Alternating from side to side, he soon clears this stand. Green heads remain on the stalks, to ripen over the next few days, which means St. Clair can return for another canoeload later. Only Native Americans and Minnesota residents with the proper licenses are allowed to gather rice in this time-honored way, limiting the number of ricers to prevent overharvesting.

It's a job for the tough. Minnesota's monster mosquitoes swarm angrily at the disturbance. Mushy white rice worms squiggle across the harvested grains. There's little talk because of the dust and the possibility of scratchy rice beards lodging in the throat. As the sun and heat rise, St. Clair moves through the stand. His passage is barely obvious. The few bent reeds soon right themselves and the lake repairs its quiet self.

Before starting out, traditionalist St. Clair crushes a cigaret and sprinkles the tobacco over the water. It is a gift to the land and the spirits. The Army veteran, who spent more than twenty years living in the Twin Cities, returned to the reservation several years ago to stay in touch with his heritage. Keeping tradition alive remains important to him.

Such old ways are becoming rare, however, since many of the young Chippewa skip such harvest ceremonies. They trample through the rice stands and all-too-eagerly take the green as well as ready rice. But a fast-working harvester can potentially bring 300 to 500 pounds a day to a processor, earning up to one dollar a pound depending on the market.

Typical of the few hand-operated finishing operations left on the reservation, the Mah Konce drying barn is a must-see. Bob Shimek (whose Chippewa name is Ani Kikiiwanaquat or "Thunder Cloud") has operated Mah Konce for the past five years.

Located at the corner of State 200 and County 4 near Lake Goodwin, the building contains a fifty-year-old parcher, a massive drum holding up to 350 pounds of rice. As the grains are poached over an open fire, the hulls eventually flake away. After the drying, threshing then separates the hulls and chaff from the rice.

But if the rice is too green, there might only be a 40 percent or less return on quality finished rice. So patient old-time ricers such as St. Clair take their time, harvesting only the more ripened grains. They may not bring in as much for drying, but they will still get at least 70 percent firm, dried rice after the processing. Each finished pound will bring five to six dollars.

"There's no need to rush if you do it right," St. Clair smiles.

In the old days, entire Chippewa families would set up camp for several weeks near the lakes. After the crop was canoed to shore and parched, a pit was dug and lined with hides, and the rice would then be dumped in. Women and children walked on the grains to remove the outer husks in a ceremony called "dancing the rice." Finally, the grain was winnowed to remove the remaining chaff.

The sprawling White Earth Reservation is about an hour's drive east of the Minnesota-North Dakota border. One of the state's largest reservations, White Earth is a catchment of large and small lakes, swampland, farms, hamlets, and pine groves that replaced the logged-over forests. County 34 is one of the major highways south of the reservation, connecting many of the nearby resort communities. Trunk highways, such as State 200 and 92, plus county roads, lead through Chippewa lands. Nearby Detroit Lakes, with its shoreside lodges and camp-grounds, is a popular resort area forty-five minutes south of the reservation. Also nearby is Park Rapids, surrounded by reservation lands between Fish Hook and Long Lake. Park Rapids is the home of the North Country Museum of the Arts, with excellent hiking opportunities at Heartland and Northern Pine Lakes trails.

The fertile, loamy landscape of western Minnesota is a pancake legacy of Lake Agassiz, a vast prehistoric body of water formed by glacial leftovers in Canada, the Dakotas, and Minnesota. From 7900 to 7500 B.C., the lake encompassed 135,000 square miles. Lakes Winnipeg, Manitoba, and Win-nipegossis are deep remnants of Agassiz.

When you leave Fargo's Hector Field airport for Minne-sota, you immediately cross the winding, whiplashed Red River into Moorhead. The muddy Red flows northward into Canada's Lake Winnipeg, delineating the fertile basin sloping from Minnesota's central highlands into the great prairie. Durham wheat, potato, and sugar beet fields stretch toward the limitless horizon. Expanses of perky yellow sunflowers, always leaning east, point the way forward. No one ever need be lost wherever there is a sunflower crop.

After taking US 75 north out of Moorhead, follow those sunflowers straight east on County 26. During the harvest, bright-red International Harvester and jolly-green John Deere combines chew their way across the acres of wheat with the predatory appetites of giant insects. Distant chaff smudges the slow, purposeful advance of the machinery. The living grain pours into wide trailer beds of eighteen-wheeler freight trucks that pull directly onto the fields to be closer to the pickers. Groaning with full loads, the rigs return to the highway for a long haul to mills in eastern Minnesota or the Twin Cities.

Once the hunting grounds of the Sioux and other Plains tribes, the land was settled by thick-skinned—and usually sunburned—Norwegians, Swedes, Germans, and French Canadians who bent this countryside to their will. They plowed the thick prairie grasses, constructed sod houses, and sowed civilization's seeds. Bursting Butler storage bins, with the pomposity of Norman watch towers, now keep an eye over the crops.

Western Minnesota is also ruffed grouse country, where the eager Boys and Girls of Autumn gather from around the country with trusty over-and-under pump-action fowling pieces. Set to do battle with the plump birds, the orange-clad visitors strut the main streets of small towns. They chug gallons of steaming coffee in the mom-and-pop cafes before hitting the roosting sites each morning. The ritualistic bam-bam-caboom of fall's artillery along the country roads is as familiar to locals as a slamwham thunderstorm.

County 26 rushes through tiny Hitterdahl, with Senas' Lefsa Company on the north side of the highway. Lefsa, a flat potato pancake from Fjord Country, makes up in taste what it lacks in physical presence, so stop to shop while motoring through this Scandinavian stronghold. But call ahead. Hours are irregular.

Past the village is an easterly ridge that seems to catapult the traveler into Minnesota's western lake district. All of a sudden, the hills are—whump—right there, as if an imaginary line separating the valley from the highland was lifted, although the rising grade is obvious when you look in the rearview mirror.

Oaks and maples toss their comforting shade over farm lawns decorated with tiptoeing concrete deer. Painted wooden cutouts of old ladies' stooping backsides perk up flower beds rainbowed with marigolds and mums. Instead of the 1,000-acre wheatfields just to the west, smaller plots of feed corn snuggle up against the fencerows in tidy squares.

At the intersection of County 26 and US 59, turn north to Callaway, home of the Robin's Nest Cafe and Manitok Wild Rice. Bearlike, bearded Dave Reinke manages Manitok, now one of the primary buyers of the Chippewas' premium rice crop in this part of the state. The shop is delightfully airy and bright, offering such Chippewa homecrafts as good-luck bird-houses, bark teepees, heavy quilts, delicate clay pottery, and willow baskets. Of course, there are bags of rice, boxes of freshly picked berries, jars of wild plum jam, and containers of clover honey. In English, Manitok means "God of the Earth."

There's nothing that indulges the taste buds like Manitok's highbush cranberry syrup. Pouring it thickly over a stack of wild rice pancakes, especially those made by bubbly Darlene Stigsell at her family's Woodland Trails Resort, makes a feast fit for backcountry kings and queens. Like many resorts around the reservation, Woodland Trails in nearby Ogema features many such locally produced food products.

Intricately woven dream catchers hang from a tree branch in the center of the Manitok shop. A dream catcher is made from a supple twig formed into a circle. Catgut or rawhide strips make the spiderweb design, which often incorporates beads and feathers. According to Chippewa lore, the large hole in the center of each dream catcher allows in good feelings. Nightmares and bad vibes are snared by the webbing and prevented from hurting the heart.

Reinke, a naval gunner's mate in Vietnam, came back from the horror to live quietly in Minnesota. He built his own home and lived off the land for a couple of years. Chopping firewood, fishing, trapping, picking berries, leeching, and other outdoor pursuits gave him plenty of background knowledge for his current job. His blue Ford pickup is a familiar sight around the White Earth reservation, as he encourages the Chippewa to expand their craft and food markets. Ricer Denny St. Clair is one of his closest neighbors.

"Having a central place like Manitok gives many of the people here another outlet for their skills. It took a while for some of them to realize the potential, but they are gradually being won over," says Reinke. "I'm a hard-nosed German, used to forging right ahead and doing a job immediately. I had a hard time at first dealing with the tribal folks, but now I think we're over the hump," he laughs.

Reinke's eyes dart constantly over the autumn underbrush whenever he swings around Bad Medicine, Strawberry, Many Point, or any of the hundreds of other lakes around the reservation. Searching for pockets of wild chokecherries or thorn apples, especially along abandoned railroad grades, he can quickly contact one of his Chippewa suppliers to pick the fruit.

Reinke can also make arrangements for Minnesota visitors to sample a ricing experience with one of the local harvesters, depending on weather and availability of the crop. Dress casually, carry bug repellent, and be prepared to learn.

When driving through the region, be open to new experiences. Mahnomen County demonstrates the contemporary and ancient ways of the reservation. The village of Nay Tah Waush, shouldering County 4 along North Twin Lake, is in the heart of the reservation at the eastern edge of the county. An old tribal cemetery can be found along an unmarked dirt road one-half mile west of town, in a tiny glade just beyond Bad Boy Creek. To find the site, turn off the paved highway at Wadena's convenience store, drive to the edge of the village, and proceed slowly, because the plot is easy to miss.

The cemetery has twelve graves, each covered by a knee-high wooden "house" having a little window facing north, allowing the spirit of the deceased to come and go. In this same vein, at some traditional Chippewa funerals held in a Christian church, the coffin is often passed through a window rather than carried out the door. Pause here briefly and gently touch the ancient wood protecting the grave sites, where the past is still part of today.

There's little in the town of Mahnomen, on the western side of the county, that affords such contemplation. The ping and cling of rattling coins in slot machines and the flup-flupping of dealt cards at the blackjack tables make their own musical score inside the Shooting Star Casino. One of the thirteen or so tribal-owned gambling operations in Minnesota, Shooting Star is all rush and bustle. However, the facility does provide hundreds of thousands of dollars for reservation development purposes.

Many tribal members work at the site, which attracts tourists from around the Midwest. The jobs are all-important for keeping many of the younger Chippewa close to home. Spin-off money from the casino is earmarked to pay for many of the reservation's social services and to provide a jump-start for economic projects.

Some thirty or so miles north of Nay Tah Waush, along County 4 and 7, are vast paddies of cultivated wild rice. Among the largest producers in the world, Rod Skoe of Clearwater Rice harvests about 1,700 acres each year around the town of Clearbrook. Six miles to the north at Gonvick is Paul Imle's Pine Lake Wild Rice.

Using modified combines with twenty-foot cutters and tractor treads instead of front tires, the air-conditioned harvest machinery cuts wide swaths through the towering grain. In the late summer harvest, the monster machinery can be spotted plotching through the drained, muddy paddies.

The high-tech operation is a distant echo of Denny St. Clair's cedar-stick knockers. Knowledgeable chefs say they can tell the difference between hand-harvested and cultivated varieties. It is not a "good" or "bad" issue, they emphasize, simply one of taste. Hand-cultivated rice supposedly has a more nutty flavor.

The paddies provide natural cover to dozens of bird species, from mallards to teal, marsh hawks, American bittern, and the short-eared owl. Brown-gray sandhill cranes float kitelike on the sky, graceful in the air but all legs and wings on the ground. Migrating tundra swans are often seen in the vicinity during the spring and autumn. Bird-watchers are usually welcome along any of the roads around the paddies, but secure permission before you move onto private property. Clearwater and Pine Lake are used by the University of Minnesota as experimental testing stations for the capture and banding of many birds. Dr. Dan Svedarsky of the university's Crookston branch spearheads the project.

His long, lanky form is often seen striding the periphery of the rice paddies, binoculars in hand and graduate students in tow. Robert Janssen of the Minnesota Ornithological Union (612-546-4220) can provide tips on the best viewing areas. Observant farmworkers occasionally even spot shy moose stomping around the adjacent swamps, as well as bears and wolves, so hikers are encouraged to remember that the wilderness is not far away, either in geography or spirit.

Lake Itasca State Park, ringed by Clearwater County 38, is where it all begins for the Mississippi River. Only twenty-two miles north of Park Rapids by US 71, the park is one of the most popular in the state. Thousands of guests visit annually to step across the baby river as it flows out of Lake Itasca in the Headwaters State Forest. With abandon, go barefoot or wear sandals, because the water rushing over a pathway of slippery rocks is ankle deep. The lake, known to Native Americans for generations, was "discovered" by explorer Henry Schoolcraft in 1832. There is an easy 600-foot walk from the parking lot to the streamhead. Crossing the river there supposedly ensures a long life, according to Elizabeth Murray, park naturalist supervisor.

The park also is home to the state's largest white pine tree, a 250-foot-tall giant standing along Two Spot Trail.

Ancient Native Americans also ran bison off a cliff in dim pre-park days not far from the towering pine. Killed in the plunge, the animals would be used for food, clothing, and implements. The thunder of their hooves can almost be heard when you stand at the precipice, reached off County 38 near the park's Elk Lake.

Dedicated and muscled canoeists can put in at Itasca and travel 536 miles south through Minnesota on a state-designated Mississippi River route, feeling the river's expanding power with every mile traveled. That power is certainly the life force throughout western Minnesota, linking tradition to today.

In the Area

Lake Itasca State Park (Lake Itasca): 218-266-3654

Manitok Wild Rice (Callaway): 218-375-4765 or
     800-726-1863

Shooting Star Casino and Lodge (Mahnomen):
     800-453-1863

Senas' Lefsa Company (Hitterdahl): 218-962-3306

Darlene Stigsell/Woodland Trails Resort (Ogema):
     800-327-7151

Clearwater Rice (Clearbrook): 218-776-3300

Pine Lake Wild Rice (Gonvick): 218-487-5759

Minnesota Department of Agriculture (St. Paul):
     612-297-5510

Minnesota Cultivated Wild Rice Council (St. Paul):
     612-638-1955 or 800-235-8906

8 ~

Walnut

Grove

Getting there: From the Twin Cities, take State 212 west to State 4, turn south to US 14, turn west to Walnut Grove; from Mankato, take US 14 west.

Highlights: *rural countryside, Laura Ingalls Wilder homesites, historical pageant, craft shops, home cooking, sod house.*

Murray, Cottonwood, Redwood, and Brown counties in western Minnesota are pancake enough to stretch the distant horizon into another infinity. But while driving eastward from Pipestone on State 30, you'll suddenly see a depression delineating what some geologists call the Missouri and Mississippi Rivers Drainage Divide. This "gully" snakes its way out of the Dakotas, through this southwestern corner of Minnesota, and on into Iowa.

Streams feeding the system are fat now, swollen by record rains that leave adjacent fields submerged and farmers cussing and crying. Just before you drive through the hamlet of Lake Wilson, the trough can be sensed more than seen. Swoop. Up and then down, a slight dip and then almost immediately the flatlands make their presence known again. Pool-table flat, except for contemporary stands of oak and maple, along with apple orchards, wheat fields, and drainage ditches, the earth remains rough on top. Unforgiving out here, it seems always ready to revert to a more primal presence. In fact, it was only a century and a half ago—a mere sneeze in the universality of time—when there was nothing but the constant hymn of the wind, a sensuous perfume of sweet grass, and a palette of long-plumed purple avens, black-eyed Susans, prairie sunflowers, and Queen Anne's lace. Take away the windbreaks, the grain elevators, and the country stores, and the land reasserts itself for mile upon mile upon mile.

There is an old folk song that goes something like "it's a land to set ya dreamin', and the dreamin will set ya free." And dreaming there was when thousands of Norwegians, Swedes, Germans, and other land-hungry nationalities flocked to the rich soil.

Seeking their personal pot of gold at the end of whatever rainbow led them to Minnesota, they risked their lives and spirits out on this prairie. Confronted with blizzards, droughts, grasshoppers, grass fires, and disease, they survived. Turning the soil to their own uses, they moved from sod huts to frame houses, built roads and towns, and became integral to the Grand Midwestern Breadbasket. The earth gave. But, as evidenced by the rain-swollen backstreams and submerged pastureland this season, it is obvious that nature still often holds a royal flush to the farmers' two of a kind.

Slayton, located at the junction of State 30 and US 59, proclaims itself the "shopping hub of southwestern Minnesota." The main street, with parking down the median strip, has a Ben Franklin, a Suit Yourself clothing, and the usual lineup of hardware stores and drug emporiums. Even in midday, shoppers stroll the streets. The door to KISDA and KLOH radio stations is locked. The Murray County Historical Museum, 29th Street and Broadway, is open, however. Packed with antique farm equipment and house "stuff" from the settler years, the facility is open from 1:00 to 4:00 P.M. Tuesday through Sunday, Memorial Day to Labor Day.

Thanks to the Murray County Raceway, Slayton's steamy Friday nights reverberate with the roar of souped-up engines from Memorial to Labor Day. Staged by the Murray County Racing Association, hobby stock and modifieds whip around the track. Gates open like clockwork at 6:30 P.M. Preliminary hot laps start at 7:30 P.M. on the 3/8-mile dirt track located on the south side of town (follow the noise). Tickets are a mere five bucks for adults, with kids twelve and under free.

The cars blast from their starting positions, beginning promptly at 8:00 P.M. Between events, the modified and hobby stock crews from Iowa, Dakota, and Minnesota chew grit, change tires, exchange gossip and horsepower, and generally ogle the passing girls. In the light of day, the guys are clerks, carpenters, and farmhands. By a summer weekend, they are ready to play out Mario Andretti (filtered through Brando) roles with all the 1950s shadings.

At T. C.'s Repair Shop (open 9:00 A.M. to 6:00 P.M., Monday to Friday) on State 30, Mark Sanow and his mechanic, John Cumminskey, are studying the exposed guts of a 1980 Monaco nicknamed Baby Bird II, preparing for the next jousting on the nearby track. Their battered, but freshly painted, canary-colored No. 23 is plastered with Schmitz Grain sponsorship signage. Almost in the same breath, they talk plugs, tires, radiators, and cutting to the inside on that new driver up from Spencer, Iowa.

Turn north at Pete's Corner on the east side of Slayton, where State 30 and US 59 meet. Travel north on 30/59 to Lake Shetek State Park, whose heavily forested shores offer a respite from the surrounding farmland. The park includes a swimming beach, a bird sanctuary, and a pioneer cabin for exploring. Kids enjoy the canoeing and crappie fishing on the lake, one of the largest in southwestern Minnesota. A gravel public access road off State 30 leads past the Lake Shetek Baptist Church and edges down to the water, where there are private vacation homes and a bait shop.

The highways separate again near the park, with US 59 heading north. Turn back east on State 30 to Currie and visit the End-O-Line Railroad Park and Museum on County 18. This restored railroad yard is adjacent to the turgid Des Moines River, where the waterway flows southward from the cool blue-green Lake Shetek.

A Grand Trunk Western caboose, a switcher, and other rolling stock are displayed at the little park. The facility is open Memorial Day through Labor Day from 10:00 A.M. to noon and from 1:00 to 5:00 P.M. from Monday through Friday, and from 1:00 P.M. to 5:00 P.M. on Saturday and Sunday. Admission is $2 for adults, $1 for seniors, and $5 for a family. Picnic tables for spreading out brought-from-home potato salad, hot peppers, and sandwiches are available in a grove by the river.

Drive east on State 30 about fifteen miles, through Dovray and on to Westbrook. At Westbrook, turn north onto County 45, which runs directly to Walnut Grove. Population 695, the village is raw around the edges. A typical farm-belt town touched by the prairie sky, its wide streets can accommodate a fleet of semitrailers groaning with loads of corn and wheat. A century ago, the same avenues were just as comfortable with horse-drawn wagons. If you squint into the noon sun, that 100-year-old image comes alive. Blue-jeaned, pot-bellied truckers and their Bulldog Macks fade while pioneer teamsters emerge in the mind's eye. As a youngster, author Laura Ingalls Wilder lived on a nearby farm for three and a

Laura Ingalls and her family lived On the Banks
of Plum Creek *near Walnut Grove*

half years before moving with her family to the Dakota Territory in 1879.

Wilder's youth there provided inspiration for her book *Little House on the Prairie,* which was made into a successful, long-running TV show. Many of the actors and actresses who appeared in that program have visited Walnut Grove. Guests of the town are sometimes startled to be standing next to Karen Grassle (who played Ma), Melissa Sue Anderson (Mary), Katherine McGregor (Mrs. Oleson), or Alison Arngrim (Nellie Oleson).

Pick up a seventy-five-cent walking/drive brochure and map of the town at the Wilder Museum, located in an old depot near the railroad tracks at the junction of US 14 and County 45. The museum is free, open from Memorial Day through Labor Day from 10:00 A.M. to 7:00 P.M. Hours in May and September are from 10:00 A.M. to 5:00 P.M., with April and October hours from 10:00 A.M. to 3:00 P.M. Inside is a rummager's delight, with the Bible from the school Wilder attended, one of her colorful quilts, and "modern" artifacts from the TV show. A covered wagon is near the front door, perfect for kid-climbing and picture taking. A tiny Children's Chapel on the museum grounds was an 1882 Methodist Church moved to the site.

This church was truly ecumenical in origin: the local Congregational church brought over pews, the Catholic church presented an altar cloth, and the Lutherans donated windows. One can almost hear the interdenominational hymns bursting forth.

Walnut Grove is made for strolling, especially on a summer day when the cicadas are calling and the heat rises from the pavement. Youngsters pedal past on their way home from some secret play space, eager for cold lemonade. Across the street from the museum is the original Masters Hotel, now a home. The Ingalls family worked for William Masters for a time. Walk along Main Street to the little park on the north side of the avenue. Sit by the statue of young Ingalls Wilder that is perkily placed there and snap some brag-photos to show the *Little House* fans at home. Turn right on Fifth Street and go one block to the site of what was the Union Congregational Church, whose pastors were often mentioned in the stories. In 1875, the Ingalls family lived behind the church in a small house where Charles Frederick Ingalls was born on November 1. The house has since been torn down, however.

To get to the Ingalls farm, drive straight north from the museum and hotel on County 5. About one and a half miles up the asphalt is a dirt road leading to the farm, now owned by the Gordon family. Directional signs are nailed to trees on the way. Drive through the barnyard, where just beyond the farmhouse is a gate to a narrow path. This path leads to a dugout along Plum Creek where Charles and Carolyn (Pa and Ma) Ingalls and their family stayed for a winter when they first moved there. An honor-system donation is requested for the upkeep of the grounds, so drop in the requested $2. A large rock where Ingalls Wilder used to sit and daydream and the waterfall where Pa set fish traps can be seen while heading to the rude home. A bridge was built across the creek in 1974 to accommodate the visitors.

Leaving the homesite, turn right on County 5 and go about a quarter mile to a historical-site landmark praising the hard work and spirit of the early Minnesota pioneers. Framed by daffodils, the monument is backed by a cornfield, the final legacy of those who settled there. Although there is a pullover along the road for parking, watch the traffic. Grain trucks and cattle-filled semitrailers regularly swoosh past.

Another five miles up the highway is The Nature Conservancy's Wahpeton Prairie, remnant of the tall-grass landscape that Ingalls Wilder would have seen when she arrived in the area. Walking trails meander through the nearby woods along the Cottonwood River.

106

Each July, *Fragments of a Dream* is presented in an outdoor theater just west of Walnut Grove, near Plum Creek Park. Classed as one of Minnesota's top festivals, the presentation has been staged by local volunteers since 1978. Written by James Merchant, the two-act drama follows the story line of *On the Banks of Plum Creek*, using Ingalls Wilder's childhood narration. A choral concert precedes the play at 8:00 P.M., with the show beginning under the lights at 9:00 P.M. The ticket office opens at 7:00 P.M. on pageant nights. General admission is $5, with reserved seating at $6.

Back in town, stop at Delon and Donna Knudson's craft shop on US 14 and peruse the rows of woodworking that line the shelves. Gifts include handmade candle holders, yo-yos, Christmas ornaments, and dozens of dolls. The family works year-round on the items, between Donna's job as a home economics teacher and Delon's bartending and work at the Walnut Grove municipal light plant.

To get a real feel for homestead life, stop at the McCone Sod House on the Prairie, eighteen miles east of Walnut Grove, just beyond where the castlelike Meadowland Co-op grain towers blend gray into the stark blue sky. The home is one mile east and one-quarter mile south of Sanborn Corner (the junction of US 71 and US 14), along a gravel road that runs parallel to the Brown and Cottonwood county lines. Virginia and Sam McCone bought the twenty-five-acre property in 1974, when he worked as a cattle buyer while raising their own "herd" of kids: Steve, Charlie, Christy, Benton, and Tom. Katie, a black Labrador, keeps an eye on the whole operation from her perch on the farmhouse back steps.

A large sod house was built in 1987 and a smaller structure erected in 1988, a few hundred feet into the prairie beyond the contemporary farm buildings. The site is open to guests from 9:00 A.M. to 5:00 P.M. weekdays and 2:00 to 5:00 P.M. Sundays from May to Labor Day. Admission is $2.

It took McCone 350,000 pounds of sod to construct his thirty-six-foot by twenty-one-foot house in the style of an 1880 building. Beds inside are covered with buffalo-skin robes, from the family's own domestic buffalo herd. A wood stove provides wintertime heat, making it snug and comfy for bed and breakfast guests. McCone's own great-grandfather on his dad's side built a similar house while homesteading in South Dakota.

"One day, we just started cutting bluegrass turf to see if we could build a sod house," McCone says, his sunburned face turned toward the buildings. "That didn't work very well, so we got permission to go to a site south of Sanborn to cut better sod," he recalls. For measuring the two-foot-long, four- to six-inch-deep hunks, he used a footboard taken from an antique plow—just as his great-grandpop did a century earlier. Cutting 20,000 pounds of sod a day, the McCones and a young neighbor built the first building in ten weeks. "In the old days, it took two men only two weeks to construct a sod house. But we were learning as we were going," McCone explains.

The Sod House Foundation in Colby, Kansas, gave invaluable help by providing memoirs of settlers who told how they built their homes. "We never used a ruler or a plane," McCone justifiably brags. "We just stood back and looked at it, making corrections as we went along. A good sod house will stand for a long time." McCone has added some refinements for contemporary guests, such as plastered and whitewashed interior walls and a wooden floor in the big house. Overnight costs are $60 per person and $100 a couple.

The smaller house, called a "poor man's dugout," is more like an original cabin rather than the larger "rich man's soddy." With its hard-packed dirt floor and rude furnishings, the rough and rugged pioneering lifestyle becomes obvious. "People these days are always griping about something. They don't want challenge, they want security. But think how these folks lived. No TV, no Coke. But from these humble beginnings, everything got better," he says. "It was that attitude that built America, where people were trying to better their lives."

In the Area

Murray County Historical Museum (Slayton): 507-836-6533

End-O-Line Railroad Park and Museum (Currie):
    507-763-3113

Laura Ingalls Wilder Museum (Walnut Grove): 507-859-2358;
    507-859-2155 (off-season)

Wilder Pageant Committee (Walnut Grove): 800-554-1707
    or 507-859-2174

McCone's Sod House Bed & Breakfast (Sanborn):
    507-723-5138

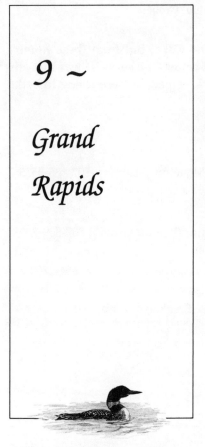

9 ~

Grand Rapids

Getting there: From the Twin Cities, take US 169 for the 3.5-hour drive north to Grand Rapids. Distance is about 200 miles.

Highlights: *snowmobiling, cross-country skiing, Forest History Center, canoe-making, hiking, summertime and ice fishing, fur-trading rendezvous.*

History is not seasonal around Grand Rapids.

Three feet of snow pillows the landscape. A winter may see as much as eighty-four inches blanketing Minnesota's North Woods, with temperatures crashing to a minus forty degrees—make that minus ninety degrees when the harsh wind chill is factored into the hot-toddy equation. Temperatures like that were enough to ban thermometers in old-time logging camps. There would have been mutiny if the timbermen knew how cold it was.

After all, they had to eat their noon dinners outside, regardless of the cold. "We're huddled around the fire. The beans on the plate are boiled on the fire side and frozen on the other," one logger wrote home at the turn of the century.

It's easier today for us contemporary types, especially when driving out to the Forest History Center, just a five-minute jaunt from downtown Grand Rapids. A car heater makes you forget that the raw wind is clutching at the outside air. As you step out onto the parking lot, spoken words turn into frozen vocabulary, hanging there . . . able to be heard only when the spring thaw arrives. Or so the Minnesota joke goes.

Clumps of new snow drape the spruce and birch on your quick stroll to the interpretive center, where cookies and hot cider await. Cross-country skiers, oblivious to the cold, swoosh past, heading for one of the two trails that loop through the groves and tamarack marshes surrounding the rustic complex. Their legs and arms sweep in graceful unison, moving much faster than several bundled-up snowshoers clomping along like forlorn bears.

The Forest History Center, one of eighteen Minnesota Historical Society sites around the state, offers a peek back into the past. The rough, ribald, and rowdy world of logging is augmented with displays on the environment, Native Americans, and contemporary woodland issues.

Open daily in the winter, the place bustles with regular classes on snowshoe-making, candle-illuminated or moonlit cross-country skiing, and other seasonal activities. In the summer, a logging camp is open, with costumed intepreters telling how life was on the frontier more than ninety years ago. In 1900, at the peak of the state's timber-cutting days, one billion board feet of lumber was taken from the Minnesota forests. In the years from 1830 to 1930, the harvest totaled 68 billion board feet. A film in the center shows the last big timber drive, during which more than a million board feet of timber were floated 100 miles along the Little Fork River to the sawmills. Viewers stand behind a jumble of piled logs, reminiscent of a jam, to get the feel of racing downriver. The Little Fork is about forty miles north of Grand Rapids.

This second Saturday of December is a special time, when the entire logging camp reopens to guests for a busy Christmas program that highlights winter life in the woods. A team of oversize draft horses pulling a sleigh packed with huzzahing, apple-cheeked kids pushes past a crowd of strolling visitors bundled like outer-space travelers. Massive hooves push out the snow better than a truck plow. The jingling of harness bells lightens the air. So who cares about the temperature.

To get to the Forest History Center from downtown Grand Rapids, take US 169 south one mile to Golf Course Road, turn right (west) and take another right on County 76. A sign about 200 yards down the road on the right announces the complex entrance. The drive takes about five minutes. A ten-minute route consists of a drive west on US 2 from downtown, with a left turn (south) on County 63, then left on County 76 to the entrance. Both routes are also well-marked with brown-and-white directional signage. A bonus sight along US 169 is the sprawling Blandin Paper Company, which produces glossy paper stock for the international market.

Employing 1,500 people, the firm is one of the major businesses in Grand Rapids, a proud lumber town from its rough-cut beginnings in the last century. The company sponsors the Vinterloppet Nordic Ski Races on the Sugar Hills Cross Country Ski Trails, a test of stamina for racers pushing through twelve- and fourteen-kilometer freestyle runs and a fourteen-kilometer classic-technique race. The races are usually held in late January.

But today isn't the day for scooting over the snow. It's back to history at the Forest Center. The quick drive from town is its own time machine. Daily winter hours at the center are noon to 4:00 P.M., from October 16 to Memorial Day, while daily summer hours are from 10:00 A.M. to 5:00 P.M. Admission is free in the winter—with $3 for adults and $1 for youngsters five to sixteen in the summer.

To satisfy a voracious national appetite for lumber those long generations ago, thousands of men and women labored from sunup to sundown six days a week from November to March. Working in intense cold, with snow piled up to the cabin eaves, they would chop and saw their way into the spring, preparing logs for the river rush downstream to the mills. The history center brings to life all that gritty realism. There were at least 350 such similar "jack" camps in northern Minnesota in the early 1900s.

A heavily bearded man bangs open a bunkhouse door, scratching through his heavy red underwear. He shrugs forward into the cold and yawns. Songs and laughter follow him outside. A cluster of mittened/stocking-capped kids stop to stare. "Hoppy Yule, kinder," he roars. The youngsters continue watching wide-eyed as he strolls up a snow-trampled path to a cookhouse, where the heavenly scent of roasting turkey is a temptation. Since the interpreters are acting out a Christmas holiday, they don't have to "work" and subsequently pretend they are on a rare day off.

A typical holiday would mean washing clothes, sleeping, playing cards, singing, and eating—exactly what the performers do for the center's pre-Christmas program. They portray the foremen, timber cutters, teamsters, cooks, blacksmiths, and other typical occupations found around such a camp.

Even women get in on the act. Becky Jennings acts as head cook Beatrice, a young Swedish-American girl seeking to earn money to buy some land and capture a husband. In real life, Jennings is a local housewife who enjoys the chance to portray someone else. She is spending her day checking woodstoves, washing dishes, and talking with center guests as if they were her lumberjack friends. No "belly robber," a camp nickname for lousy cook, "Beatrice" cooks up a storm for a table-groaning holiday meal to be shared by the interpreters after the center closes. Now, she lets a couple of contemporary toddlers share a fresh cookie.

Outside, camp life continues. Bill Carpenter shapes a horseshoe at his forge in the blacksmith shop. Drew Davis pretends he is a clerk, checking financial figures in the "wanigan," the camp office. Two burly jacks convince several teenage boys to try their hand at sawing logs. The men hold a huge crosscut with teeth straight from a saber-toothed tiger. A couple of the high-schoolers tackle the project on a dare from their buddies, strutting up to the saw and log, spitting on their hands, and going to it. Within minutes, their faces are red and they are out of breath.

"Hmm," one lumberjack actor nudges the other. "Think they'll make it out here?" The other replies with a grin, "It won't take 'em long. We'll get 'em in shape." Both interpreters, men in their sixties who have hungry wood-fired stoves that need constant feeding at home, pick up the saw. They swing into action and slice the two-foot-diameter log as easily as if cutting margarine. Sheepishly, the cool school guys take a bow and depart quickly. If they had signed on with a timber camp years ago, all the goods they bought at the company store would have been deducted from their fifteen dollars per week. They couldn't even collect their wages until midsummer, when the logs were floated to the mill and the results tallied.

In the bunkhouse, several men are playing guitars and singing. The heavy smell of wet wool and woodsmoke combine in a North Woods incense that clings to clothes and hair. Oblivious to the Eau de Timber, a cluster of enthralled guests surround the musicians. The warmth of the season is real.

Robert (Skip) Drake, the center's director, proudly leads guests through the displays. Attractive lighting touches the corners, easing visitors into an imaginary world, but one based on the reality of history and environment. Separated into four major groups, the exhibits tell the life of the forest. The first section studies its evolution. Drake points out a ten-inch spruce stump that was snapped off by the last glacier to rumble over the Grand Rapids area 10,000 years ago. "Genetically, this is the same type of tree we have here today," he explains.

The second gallery focuses on the symbiotic relationship between the forest and the Native American. Ojibwa tribal members from nearby Leech Lake Indian Reservation helped construct a twelve-foot-diameter wigwam that is a centerpiece exhibit in the center's main building. The snug, five-foot-high structure is made of ash bark and maple saplings. Photos and artifacts tell the fascinating story of how the Indians made the woodlands their own.

The third gallery depicts the European influence on the forest, with extensive details on the logging industry. Three computer terminals have a bevy of children around them. One machine allows the kids to test (and probably remember) a lumberjack vocabulary (sans swear words) on the interactive screens. Another allows players to "sign on" for winter work in a camp and trace their earnings. A third machine lets the participants become camp foremen, who must make important decisions about how to manage the camp and the logging crew. A miscalculation will mean the player loses all his or her money.

In the next gallery, viewers confront forest issues of the 1990s and play interactive games that let them become fire wardens or answer questions on the environment. When the center reopens all its grounds in the summer, a 1930s-era ranger station complete with fire tower can be toured, as well as the entire turn-of-the-century logging campsite.

Grand Rapids and other northern Minnesota towns revel in the snow. Sure, there are grumbles about the weather down at the First Grade diner where Mary Jo Hendricks holds sway. The restaurant is located in the Old Central School. Now a county museum, as well, the school building, 10 N.W. 5th Street, is hard to miss even when drifts are nose-deep. The imposing red-brick structure is at the intersection of State 2 and US 169, convenient for a quick dash inside for a Bunyan-size slice from one of Hendricks's apple pies. An accompanying cup of thick, heavy coffee wards off the chill.

Snowmobiling is one of the easier ways to see the Grand Rapids area when the winter wind is sculpting drifts across the country roads. Plows regularly take care of the highways, but to really plunge into the North Woods zest for wintertime living, rev up the ol' power sled and hit the trail.

The Taconite Trail originates at the Itasca County Fairgrounds in Grand Rapids, where there is plenty of free parking for cars, trucks, and trailers. Since 1986, thousands of Midwestern snowmobilers have launched off on the 170-mile "Great Northern Expressway" as it is sometimes called. The state's longest snowmobile corridor goes through some of the most rugged up-country woods in the northern United States.

Forty feet wide in some places, with steel suspension bridges across the many streams and rivers on the route, the trail connects Grand Rapids with Ely, Tower-Soudan, and other northern urban areas. Side routes spiderweb to Chisholm, Hibbing, Virginia, and Eveleth. The main leg and its spur trails cut through parts of the Superior and Chippewa national forests; the George Washington, Bear Island, Kabetogama, Sturgeon River, Koochiching, and other state forests; and the Bear Head Lake State Park.

Talk about country driving! The snowmobile "road" cuts deep into moose country, skirts such old open-pit mines as the Grand Canyon vista of the Hull-Rust hole in Nashwauk (twenty miles east of Grand Rapids on US 169), soars over

116

granite outcroppings, and drops deep into birch-shaded valleys. By the time the driver has made it to the end point at Ely, machinery vibrations have really loosened up the backside.

Maintained by the Minnesota Department of Natural Resources, the Taconite Trail is free. Other trails in the state are maintained by local clubs through a grant-in-aid program paid for by the state's $30 three-year registration fee and three-fourths of 1 percent of the unrefunded state gas tax. The United States Forestry Service and the state park system also take care of their own trails. Itasca County has some 800 miles of snow trails, augmenting the 12,000 miles of snowmobile trails crisscrossing the state. Minnesota also honors the registrations of out-of-state snowmobilers in a reciprocal agreement, so free use is for everyone.

About forty-five miles north of Grand Rapids, a panting snowmobiler finds the Swamp Siders Clubhouse, where volunteers staff a kitchen and repair shop from 10:00 A.M. to late evening on Fridays, Saturdays, and Sundays during the season. By road, the site can be reached by driving east on US 169 to Taconite and then north on County 7 to County 52. The forty- by sixty-foot clubhouse is two miles east on 52. It's a friendly, smoky place, packed with folks in tight black-leather snowmobile outfits and sweatshirts. Helmets, gloves, boots, and other gear are piled in clumps by arriving clubs. At any one time on the weekend, from 100 to 120 snowmobiles are parked in the lot, with groups arriving and departing constantly. Anybody with a necktie is definitely out of place and looked upon with great suspicion.

All the food at the Swamp Siders is homemade, with heated arguments over whose chili or vegetable or ham-and-bean soup is the best. The only way out of the dilemma is to have a hearty portion of each, plus a couple of Polish sausages, three cheeseburgers, and a hot dog . . . because all that fresh air causes grizzly-size hungries. Food is served until about 5:00 P.M., with microwaved pizza afterwards. Since the place is volunteer-run, it usually closes between 10:00 P.M. and midnight. Near-beer, the 3.2 type, is available.

For after-hours emergencies, phone numbers of nearby club members are posted on the door and a public phone is located near the front entrance. An eighth of a mile north of the clubhouse on County 52 is another phone outside the Scenic Pines grocery store and gas station, which is open from 7:00 A.M. to 7:00 P.M.

Clem Lehrer still rides his Yamaha Phazer II at age seventy. One of the organizers of the Swamp Siders, he brags that the club's repair shop can fix just about anything but a broken heart. The retired postal employee enjoys flying along the Taconite Trail. "When the trees start going by in a blur, I keep thinking that if I hit one, it will hurt for a long time." But he neglects to say if he ever slows down.

Grand Rapids annually hosts a Snowmobile Hall of Fame, honoring individuals who have made significant contributions to the sport. The awards program is usually held in the Sawmill Inn, followed by a weekend of barbecues, trail-grooming exhibitions, snowmobile races, club displays, and other activities.

Yet even in frosty Grand Rapids, all that snow does eventually melt and the country roads are clear again. It never fails. Spring arrives in an explosion of daffodils, wildflowers, and robins. Then is the time to visit the Hafeman Boat Works in Bigfork, north of Grand Rapids about forty miles. Bill Hafeman's granddaughter Christie and her husband, Ray Boessel, Jr., still make birchbark canoes in the traditional Native American manner. The elder Hafeman started constructing voyageur freight canoes and Chippewa tribal long-nose models in 1921, selling them to outdoors enthusiasts from around the country. The Boessels took over the firm in 1981 and still make canoes the good old-fashioned way: no nails or glue.

Making canoes at Hafeman Boat Works

The couple has made only one concession to modernity: a permanent polyurethane pitch has replaced the old tar pitch. The Boessels make the canoes with birchbark as an outer skin and rot-resistant cedar for the inner framework. Spruce roots provide the sinew for threading the canoe together, and sap from spruce or pine is mixed with charcoal and bear grease to seal seams and holes.

Canoes used by the French voyageurs sometimes reached thirty-seven feet long and could carry close to three and a half tons of trade goods or pelts. Twenty-six-footers were paddled by six men and could hold two tons of freight and all the traders' supplies for six weeks. In the past decade, the Boessels have made about 150 canoes, ranging in length from twenty-six feet to thirteen feet. They also make ten-, eight-, six-, and five-inch models for the collector.

Their small shop is along the south bank of the Bigfork River, one of the major French trading routes through upper Minnesota in the 1600s and 1700s. Several of the Boessels' newly made canoes are displayed on the east side of State 6, across from County 14. To drive to Bigfork from Grand Rapids, take US 2 west to Deer River. Continue north thirty miles on State 6 to the town. If the Boessels aren't too busy, they will offer a tour of the building and explain how the canoes are constructed. As the tannin-brown river gurgles past, still more canoes bob gently from their dock alongside the shop. They tug at the moorings as if to escape to the past.

Tomahawks, muzzleloaders, and skinning knives are the weapons of choice at the White Oak Rendezvous in Deer River the first weekend in August. That's when 1,000 history fans from around the United States and Canada reenact a fur-trading rendezvous. Bluegrass, cajun, jigging, clogging, and traditional Native American music and dance are featured. Service organizations from the neighborhood organize the food service. From 100 to 150 tents are set up, along with a stage in the woods for acoustic music. The event is held at the White Oak Fur Post on State 6 North, at the junction with US 2, fifteen miles west of Grand Rapids. The rendezvous brings together fur traders, hunters, British and Scottish military, Native Americans, and all sorts of other appropriately garbed characters straight out of the late 1700s.

There is hardly a better way to learn history than by wandering the grounds, talking with the colorful reenacters, and observing the day-to-day life of another era. The participants might include a bank clerk acting as a French voyageur or a housewife in the role of a trader's Ojibwa wife. They stick to the appropriate speech, foods, and festivities. No wristwatches, canned sardines, or boom boxes here.

Tickets are $6 for adults and $3 for school kids. Youngsters seven and under are free. A modern campground for guests' RVs, tents, or campers is available near the grounds at $5 per night. According to the organizers, the camping idea is to encourage families to stay for all three days of the event. For even more of a total experience, a family of four can be shown around the post by a costumed interpreter for a twenty-four-hour living experience. Mom, Dad, and tykes can sleep in a tepee or under a canoe for a North Woods Fantasy Suite feel for only $150. The host/guide teaches them survival skills and lets them cook breakfast over an open fire. Participants can even dress like the other reenacters if they wish.

During the summer, the re-created fur post is open Tuesdays, Wednesdays, and Thursdays from July to mid-August. Admission is $3, with kids seven and under free. The site consists of eighty hilly acres of oak, pine, cedar, tamarack, and birch, with a mile-long handicap-accessible nature trail that can be used all year. The plants on the route are labeled in French, Ojibwa, and English, telling how they were used for medicine, food, or shelter in the 1700s. Plenty of benches are scattered about the grounds to ease tired feet.

In the off-season, black bear, deer, and other wildlife reoccupy the remote site, a mile outside Deer River, a town of only 800 persons. The fur post itself consists of a blacksmith shop, root cellars and gardens, the Northwest Company store, and living quarters for the clerk, voyageurs, and *bourgeois*. The latter was the post's senior representative for the Montreal-based trading company. A building for constructing birchbark canoes is also on the grounds, where off-duty voyageurs could repair their craft or assemble new ones during the summer.

During the days when the post is open to the public, an adobe oven for baking fresh bread sends its heavenly scents above the breeze. Sweet and sourdough loaves sell for $1 to $2, depending on their size. A black-powder firing range is also available for competition and shooting exhibitions.

The first rendezvous at Deer River was held in 1989, before the post was constructed. Since then, $500,000 has been spent for upgrades, says a proud Perry Vining, "bourgeois" of the group whose board of directors go by their vintage 1798 titles. Improvements included dredging a river and adding a wharf where canoes are docked. Fronted by a cedar palisade to camouflage the post from State 6, the main buildings are inside a 150-by-150-foot stockade. The smokehouse, blacksmith shop, and voyageurs' quarters are outside the wall, near the entrance where guests enter. Typical of the period, placement of these buildings protects the post in case of fire. Apparently, blacksmiths were notorious for burning down the buildings in which they worked.

White Oak is managed by a nonprofit organization that works closely with the state historical society, explains Vining. "People get a real flavor of the era, walking from area to area and comparing how life was different among the various occupations at a trading post." The project is funded by private foundations and individuals, not by the state, Vining emphasizes. The original White Oak fur post, about a mile southeast of the re-created site, is on the National Register of Historic Places. However, it is privately owned and not open to the public. During World War II, fields in the vicinity provided grassy landing sites for fledgling pilots. Since the 1940s, the entire area has slowly been reclaimed by the forest.

From July 21 to August 1, 1995, the White Oak fur post will host the national Midwest Rendezvous, sanctioned by the Muzzleloader and Rifle Association. The White Oak rendezvous will follow immediately afterwards.

It is obvious that the Grand Rapids area is history conscious, with or without the snow.

In the Area

1000 Grand Lakes Visitor and Convention Bureau (Grand Rapids): 800-472-6366

Forest History Center (Grand Rapids): 218-327-4482

First Grade Restaurant (Grand Rapids): 218-326-9361

White Oak Fur Post (Deer River): 218-246-9393

Swamp Siders Clubhouse: 218-245-3222

Hafeman Boat Works, c/o Ray Boessels, Jr. (Bigfork): 218-743-3709

10 ~

Superior

National

Forest

Getting there: From the Twin Cities take I-35 north to Duluth (147 miles) and pick up State 61. Just follow the signs in downtown Duluth near the Armory. Continue north on 61 along the Lake Superior shoreline to Tofte, a drive of about eighty miles.

Highlights: *Pine forests, small towns, hiking, bears, camping, canoeing, moose, hiking, rugged shoreline, and more hiking.*

When you drive north on State 61 on a frost-tinged day in October the waters of Lake Superior chug-clug like thick, brown-black molasses against the gray rocks to the right. There is hardly anything colder than that lake, even in mid-summer. Superior is the largest body of fresh water in the world at 350 miles long and 160 miles wide, and it never warms up. It seems like one vast permanent ice cube.

Even Etienne Brule, who explored the coastline in 1616 via canoe, supposedly exclaimed to his voyageur paddlers, "Oh la la! Que c'est froid!" ("Wow, this is cold!") The crew responded more emphatically, "Bigre! Que c'est glace!" (loosely translated, according to Prof. Jean-Pierre LaFouge of Marquette University, "Boss, this water is damn cold!").

The winter of 1993/1994 saw the entire lake freeze over for the first time since March 3, 1978, according to satellite reports from the National Oceanic and Atmospheric Administration. And as a Minnesota fisheries spokesman said, looking out his window in Duluth, "Yep, it's frozen as far as I can see."

To the northeast, a good twenty miles by seasonal ferry-boat from Grand Portage, is Isle Royale National Park. The island is a haven for wolves, deer, hikers, campers, and the occasional stray hermit. Isle Royale (considered within Michigan's lake jurisdiction) is over the horizon, however, and unseen from where you drive. A stray gull provides a darting peripheral movement over the raw, hard waters. An ore freighter is spotted several miles offshore, its bow lumbering heavily into the frosty foam. In another month, the freighter traffic will be stalled because of the ice floes.

Since winter is creeping stealthily down from the Canadian wilds as you drive northward, the tourists have mostly departed and US 61 beyond Duluth is practically devoid of any moving object weighing less than two tons. This is truck time along Minnesota's eastern rim, with loggers, ore haulers, and other big rigs grunting their way up and down along the sharp rim of Lake Superior.

Small towns, mostly bait-shop and gas-pump places, swish past . . . separated by miles and miles of pine trees. Men in orange hunting caps stand outside the infrequent roadside pit stops, as if they were displaced lawn jockeys waiting to hold the reins of a panting horse. If you should pull over to get your windows washed, you'd hear—at no extra charge—polite conversation about the (perceived) lousy deer-hunting season, followed by heated commentary on the inability (close to the truth) of the Minnesota Vikings to carry a football more than four yards without fumbling.

The leaf-fluttered lawn of the Forest Service ranger station abuts the highway on the southside of Tofte. The parking lot is full of swamp-green and mud-brown panel trucks and pickups used by the park service to patrol the woods looming to the left of the road. Only about 400 people live in the village, with its rustic cabins and house trailers lining the highway. Several gas stations and convenience stores service the community. The town celebrated its 100th anniversary in 1993, with a 10K run and a wilderness run/walk through the forest. There were no reports of anyone nibbled on by picnicking bears.

Tofte is relatively undiscovered by the backcountry traveler, unlike the more widely known Gunflint District, which is to the north and east and closer to Grand Marais. The Gunflint Trail there is actually a sixty-three-mile-long asphalt-paved road lined with resorts and restaurants. Yet Tofte still logs in about 20,000 guests during the height of the camping/fishing season between May and Labor Day. Visitors should check in at the Tofte Forest Service information center to secure permits, maps, and other information about the flora and fauna of the region, which abuts the more challenging camping aspects of the Boundary Waters Canoe Area Wilderness (BWCAW), the largest wilderness preserve east of the Rockies.

Assistant Ranger Terry Eggum is one of several Forest Service personnel quick to help with questions about driving in the region. "For somebody not used to off-road driving or driving along washboard gravel roads and not the pavement, the first time into the woods might be unnerving," he said. But he agreed that it doesn't take long to catch onto maneuvering through the interior.

Generally, the woods are safe if common sense is used and the proper care is taken to avoid trouble, even on a day trip. Travel only on a full tank of gas, be sure spare tires are in good shape, and carry emergency gear (flashlight, extra blanket, matches, some food). Leave word at the ranger station when you are going into the area, inform the staff of your proposed route and timetable, and be sure to let someone there know when you return. Be aware that this is wilderness and not a zoo. Don't feed the critters. Occasionally, black bears will raid a campsite, so bag and tie foods on a high limb—well out of reach of any wandering 450-pound teddy looking for free teatime munchies.

Remember that hunting is allowed throughout the federally administered forest, with Minnesota Department of Natural Resources regulations applying on the specifics of taking grouse, deer, or other game. Wear brightly colored clothing when hiking and don't wear animal costumes, even if you belong to a Moose or Elk lodge.

Every two years, moose hunting season opens. The next round is scheduled for 1995. For those with Robin Hood and Daniel Boone inclinations, bow and gun season for black bear generally fires off in early September.

With all that in mind, happy driving.

The afternoon is already dying as my 4x4 truck aims into the dark interior of the Superior National Forest. Late October is well past goose migration, and no self-respecting mallard is within 500 miles of our campsite at Crescent Lake. The Minnesota wilderness seems impenetrable, with its thick walls of jack pine rearing up on both sides of County 2. About a mile or so past Tofte, the road turns north off US 61. If I stay on 61, I'll spot Canada in another hour or so.

Soon it will be the prime hours for deer-spotting, as the soft-eyed forest creatures edge out of the woodlots for evening grazing. Sometimes, punk deer with grudges leap in front of headlights as night descends, to scare the beejeebers out of any drowsing passing motorist.

A snowshoe rabbit, changing from its summer brown to winter white, bounds across the two-lane asphalt just before the roadway turns into gravel about two miles further into the forest. Skittering into the trees, the rabbit is quickly lost to sight. Two crows hack a message through the nippy air, a telegraph of alert that our truck is coming into their domain.

The sky is brilliantly blue, even in the afternoon, a perfect backdrop to the green pines and the wind-stripped branches in the stands of oaks. Driving through the Tofte Ranger District in the Superior forest is a step into the good old days. Now, as then, the rugged terrain, remote camping, and general wildness test the mettle of any traveler. There is the challenge and privacy of end-of-season adventuring. Not many other campers care to brave the nighttime frost at this time of year.

Our Crescent Lake campground is one of the more remote in the Tofte District, some twenty-five miles inland from the lake. The trip takes at least an hour of careful driving once you turn off the main highway. Exit on County 2, also called the Sawbill Trail. The road cuts almost straight north to Sawbill Lake on the border of the BWCAW, where no vehicles are allowed. Six miles up the Sawbill is the Blister Rust Test Site, where travelers can learn about that tree-killing disease.

To get to Crescent Lake, turn right off the Sawbill onto Forest Service Road (FSR) 170, which meanders northeast. Drive carefully, because going too fast on the rough roadway surface could result in a rock pinging through a gas tank, a flat tire, or another unnecessary and unwanted misadventure.

It is also possible to reach Crescent Lake via County 4, nicknamed the Caribou Trail. This road is about three miles north of tiny Lutsen, a village twelve miles up the Lake Superior shoreline from Tofte. Stock up on groceries in either small town. Turn left on the marked Caribou Trail and revel in the first six miles of paving before lurching onto the hard gravel. Take that winding road to FSR 170 (which rims Lichen

Lake) and continue the five-mile drive west to Crescent Lake. By then, you've seen enough pine trees to last a lifetime.

Another thirteen miles up the road, the Sawbill bisects FSR 170 near an abandoned Civilian Conservation Corps camp that dates from the 1930s. Near the crumbling buildings, a sign there relates the region's logging history, indicating that Minnesota once had more than 2,500 miles of railroad tracks serving the logging camps. There were 3,000 cars and 200 locomotives in operation during the peak of the turn-of-the-century cutting years.

Somewhere in the dense forest nearby, according to local legend, is an intact logging train still run by a ghostly crew. On dark nights, the train's eerie whistle can still be heard approaching . . . closer . . . and closer . . . and closer. Many a usually brave and believable backwoods adventurer swears that a rush of air, the powerful scent of boiler smoke, and the rumble of wheels mark the passing of skeletal spirits through their campsite.

Since we didn't know this until leaving the Tofte several days later, our tent is pitched with a minimum of fuss, gear spread around with all the appropriate anti-bear precautions, and it is time for tossing a line into the lake for supper. Unfortunately, the walleye laugh at our lures and seem reluctant to leap immediately into the waiting frying pan. So it is to be beans and their sardine cousins for supper. Even with our lack of a catch the first afternoon, there could still be great fishing in the district as long as the angler has a boat and the correct bait. Shoreline fishing is harder.

According to a passing motorist, a logger who lives in town, moose tracks were spotted earlier in the day near our campground. Up early the next morning, we spot the washtub-size cloven hoofprints fluting the sandy roadside before they trail into the underbrush and pine. But no other signs of the massive beasts are obvious during our four-day stay,

A moose breakfasts on delicious aquatic plants

although other loggers in the area report seeing several moose gallomping down one of the nearby forest roads. They were probably on the way to some pre-dawn woodsy coffee-klatsch. The moose . . . not the loggers.

October is still peak hunting time, with ruffed grouse at the top of the gourmet menu, so an occasional pop-pop of a shotgun is heard in the distance as marksmen (and women) try their dinner-collecting skills. However, only a few tough grouse hunters still roam the Tofte woodlands. Most travelers generally stick to State 61, not venturing inland as the leaves fall and the hint of snow is in the air. Subsequently, a country roads expedition here is a combination of peaceful driving, excitement, and fun. Especially in a 4x4 vehicle.

Weather conditions need to be monitored closely in the forest, with thermometer fluctuations simply a natural state of accepted affairs. Sometimes Minnesota's Mother Nature springs (no pun intended) surprises. A beautiful autumn day can hover at seventy degrees, then plunge forty-five degrees in the evening, with twelve inches of snow by morning. Autumn campers are advised to pack extra socks, down-filled sleeping bags, and other rugged-weather gear. With such precautions, there should not be any problem. We even brought a little tent heater to help ward off the chill.

The Tofte district is great for exploring, with a maze of logging roads that challenge even the toughest vehicle. However, many of the older roads are impassable in the summer because of the wirelike puckerbrush that reaches eight to twelve feet high. Yet in the winter, trails can be built almost anywhere. Loggers often mark a path across a tamarack swamp and drive with ease over the ice.

Motorists are warned to stay on marked trails, however. First, it is dangerous to get too far off the beaten track because of the possibility of an emergency. Second, wide tires can tear up off-road grade and cause massive erosion, which is frowned upon by anyone with a sense of preservation and love of the outdoors. Motorists seeking thrills can find just as much adventure on some of the so-called "roads" as on any unmarked passage. Washboard rides and jouncing over potholes big enough to swallow a bus can shake the daylights out of a driver and passengers. So remember to buckle up—a safety practice that cuts down the jostling.

But feel free to plunge mooselike into the woods on an existing road, if you will. One trail (FSR 384) that is particularly exciting cuts along the west side of Whitefish Lake, on the far edge of the Superior National Forest. The pathway slashes through the undergrowth by Organ and Bone lakes before dead-ending against a thick wall of brush. Without a sharp cutting hook, no vehicle smaller than a tank could continue. The brush can also rip off mirrors, antennas, and paint with the finesse of a black bear going after a cooler bursting with bologna. Heavy snow from previous seasons makes the brush bend over little-used trails, causing an even tighter squeeze.

And to think folks in the Tofte station suggested that particular run, after I had asked for a tough route, "one not too easy." Well, at least the guy was dead-on when it came to challenge. The forest wins that match and we turn back, in reverse for several hundred yards before finding a space wide enough for turning around.

FSR 357 from Harry Creek to the junction of 1224 is another harrowing trip. A rocky roadbed guarantees a bouncy, bottom-banging ride through a timber cut and over washed-out culverts. Grunting, the truck manages to traverse bumper-deep Wilson Creek with full 4x4 in gear before gaining the relative comfort of "better surfaced" roads on the far bank. Getting stuck here means a long walk out for help, or the hope that a passing logger can throw a chain over a bumper to winch out a waterlogged vehicle. Such thoughts notwithstanding, it is sometimes best to downshift, rev, and roar through the Olympic-size obstacle.

For good reason, a ridge on FSR 166 was dubbed Heartbreak Hill by turn-of-the-century lumbermen whose horses had to struggle up a steep grade while hauling tons of logs. Many a good Percheron supposedly did not complete the "heartbreaking" tug upward to the summit.

Taking 346 from 166 to old familiar 170, you pass the moose haven of Fourmile Lake. According to sharp-eyed woodsworkers, a herd of moose resides in the surrounding swamps and thickets. Hikers and motorists are warned to stay out of the area during rutting season earlier in the autumn because the usually bashful bulls have been known to charge anything that moves. There's nothing like being pursued down a narrow forest road by a 1,500-pound, seven-foot-tall, snorting, drooling animal with palmated antlers spreading six or more feet from tip to tip. It's an adrenalin-pumping gut feeling, akin to getting your dream date home late on the first date and finding her dad waiting up to have a word with you.

Primitive camping is allowed in the Superior National Forest, which means pulling over just about anywhere there is rare open space to pitch a tent. However, it is recommended that campers stay at a developed or dispersed camping area, because there is water, flat space, and waste and toilet facilities. Fees ($6 to $7.50 for one night) are collected on an honor system at developed sites, paid daily at the entrance to the campgrounds. Several sites are managed by concessionaires who collect fees on a regular basis. At the free, dispersed sites, waste must be disposed of properly or returned to a dump site. A fire ring also has to be maintained. Rangers vigorously enforce all the rules, both for safety and environmental protection.

Once you're in the forest, a campfire session is a perfect ending to a day of moseying through mooseland. Although an early turn-in is necessary, since the evening quickly turns to bitter frost and a warm sleeping bag beckons, there is the last chance to grab a clear look at the starry skies. Savor the stillness and imagine that no one else is around for 1,000 miles.

For detailed information and maps prior to heading to the Superior National Forest, contact the US Forest Service, Eastern Region, 310 West Wisconsin Avenue, Milwaukee, WI 53203. 414-297-3693.

In the Area

U.S. Forest Service Ranger Station, Superior National
Forest (Tofte): 218-663-7280

Boundary Waters Canoe Area Wilderness: 218-720-5324
or 800-745-3399

Grand Portage-Isle Royale Transportation Line: 715-392-2100

Isle Royale National Park: 906-482-0984

Minnesota Department of Natural Resources: 612-296-6157
or 218-723-4768

Gunflint Trail Association: 800-338-6932

Tip of the Arrowhead Association: 218-387-2524
or 800-622-4014

Heart of the Arrowhead Association: 218-353-7359

Tower-Soudan Chamber of Commerce: 218-753-2301

Lake Vermilion Resort Association: 800-648-5897

Lutsen-Tofte Tourism Association: 218-663-7804

International Wolf Center (Ely): 800-ELY-WOLF

11 ~

Mille Lacs Lake- Brainerd

Getting there: From the Twin Cities, take US 10 northwest to US 169 north to the shore of Mille Lacs Lake, then angle west on State 18 to Brainerd. Or take US 10 to State 371 at Little Falls and on to Brainerd.

Highlights: *resorts, golfing, beaches, fishing, supper clubs, Lumbertown U.S.A., Native American museums, excursion boats, swimming, loafing, and catching up with life.*

Mille Lacs Lake-Brainerd is Paul Bunyan country, where lakes dimple the undulating landscape, tinseling the earth with their sparkle and wink. Every corner has another vista, another overlook. The country roads traveler expects to see the giant woodsman and his equally steroidal ox, Babe, crunching their way across the treetops. To be sure, Paul and his brawny beast are there, all right—in the history, legends, and gift shops of the lake country of upper central Minnesota.

There is Bunyanesque competition between towns out here. Brainerd has a fifty-foot-high, hand-waving Big Paul at its Paul Bunyan Center amusement park (with twenty-nine rides). Brainerd's Bunyan is seated near the entrance, saying howdy to kids as they rush toward the Paul Bunyan Miniature Golf Course and the Krazy Maze. The center is located at the corner of State 210 and 371 and is open from 10:00 A.M. to late evening daily from Memorial Day weekend through Labor Day. For the daring, the park also offers helicopter rides over the surrounding forests for a vista formerly appreciated only by bald eagles and Bunyan himself.

But for a more realistic look at lumber life, make a summertime stop at Lumbertown U.S.A. on Pine Beach Road in Brainerd. The twenty-eight-building complex is a re-creation of a logging town from the last century. However, true to the resort nature of the place, there is also a wax museum and a miniature golf course

Akeley, at the junction of State 64 and 34, presents a kneeling Paul Bunyan, with his right hand outstretched in welcome and the left holding a great ax. The woodsy hello is appropriate, because the 398-person community claims to be Paul Bunyan's birthplace, located as it is on the southern edge of the Paul Bunyan State Forest. Akeley's downtown city park, where the statue is located, has a small logging museum that opens only during the summer months.

Bemidji (some 120 miles farther north of Brainerd by taking State 18 to 371 to US 2) also has its own Paul Bunyan, promoted with hearty "we-were-first" enthusiasm. Constructed in 1937 on the wave-rumpled shoreline of Lake Bemidji, the eighteen-foot-tall Bemidji Bunyan is made of 2.5 tons of wood, steel reinforcing rods, and concrete. It will never—read *never*—blow over in our lifetime. Or at least, let's knock on wood. Locals always know that spring has officially sprung when cleaning crews show up to paint and patch the statue, giving the big guy a vigorous pre-tourist-season facial, manicure, and massage.

Let's digress for a minute on this Bunyan guy. The semi-comic folk hero of dozens of tall tales may have popped up

Bemidji's Paul Bunyan with his indigo friend

first in Quebec, where there was an actual Paul Bunyon (note the difference in spelling names). That Bunyon had a great reputation as a brawler in Canada's Papineau Rebellion against England in 1837. He later carried his fisticuffs reputation throughout Quebec and into northern Ontario as a tough logging-camp boss.

Bunyan of timber fame made his first public appearance in print in 1914, when the Red River Lumber Company put out an ad pamphlet entitled *Paul Bunyan and His Big Blue Ox*. The little piece was written and illustrated by W. B. Laughead, who gave Bunyan his shape and launched his legendary scope. Thus was a media star born. Writers such as Acel Garland, Daniel Hoffman, Dell J. McCormick, Esther Shepard,

James Stevens, Glen Rounds, Virginia Tunvey, and many others wrote stories and scholarly treatises about the bigger-than-life fella and his folklore impact.

Actually, anybody can weave a Bunyan yarn. Simply spin a taller tale than the person next to you while hunkering around an evening's fire at the Crow Wing Lake campground. Crow Wing is only about eight miles south of Brainerd, but when the night settles in with the chatter-chatter of fuzzy forest critters, stories take on vibrant lives of their own.

Sometimes called the Riviera of the North, the Mille Lacs Lake-Brainerd neighborhood exemplifies the yin and yang of northern Minnesota. On the one hand, there is the rugged woodsy image exemplified by Bunyan, with rustic cabins and smoking chimneys, narrow rural roads plunging through darkened spruce groves, and remote lakes exploding with walleye just waiting to be landed. This is the world of blue jeans and hiking boots, of red wool caps and sharpened bucksaws, of timber cutting and black bears on the run.

But on the opposite side of the getaway equation are the upscale resorts, with their crisp clean sheets, crackling fireplaces, gourmet meals, pro-designed golf greens, beach umbrellas, and husky-voiced vacationers who karaoke until 2:00 A.M. And there is the glittering pinball effect of the Ojibwa-operated Grand Casino Mille Lacs, for a Las Vegas touch on the west shore of Mille Lacs Lake.

Somewhere in the middle is the real Mille Lacs Lake-Brainerd, the one felt when the wind tiptoes through the pine branches, when bluejays laugh at the city kids learning to bait a hook, and when rain plays its rat-a-tat-tat syncopation on tent tops.

The Ojibwa (or Chippewa) called the area *minsisaigon,* which meant "everywhere lakes." Respectful of the abundant waters, they harvested fish and rice and roamed the woods seeking life-giving berries and herbs. They hunted deer, bear, and partridge. They buried their dead on the lakeshores and passed along legends about ancestral spirits who guided them in their daily chores.

French voyageurs loved the land equally as much. They were rugged, muscular types who wore bright red kerchiefs around their heads and sang ribald songs as they paddled up to 100 or more miles a day. Aptly called the *coureurs de bois* or "woods runners," they passed through Minnesota's thickets and over the portages as easily as the white-tailed deer, establishing relations with the tribes and collecting the forest bounty for an eager European market. The French took *minsisaigon* and made it *mille lacs*, which translates to "a thousand lakes." Not that they ever counted each body of water along what is now a spiderweb of country roads, but that number seemed about right for such a magnificent azure spread of life-giving liquid.

Contemporary woods runners, in their 4x4s and minivans, have it much easier, naturally, than the tough little men who blazed those first thoroughfares through the wilds. But the fresh, freeing experience felt by the Native Americans and French traders of those good old days is certainly part of today's getaway feel. Especially at night, when stars overflow in a cascade of light, framing a glowing moon giant enough even for a real Paul Bunyan.

Bunyan, as one Minnesota story relates, even built his house with open doors tall enough to allow that moon to slide through unimpeded. Out here, everything seems possible.

US 10, the main road from Minneapolis-St. Paul, slashes northwest across the state to Moorhead, where it crosses the border into North Dakota and a connection with I-94. The vacation-hungry traveler can exit US 10 at several junctions to get to Brainerd, including State 25 or State 371 at Little Falls. US 169 at Elk River leads directly to the west side of Mille Lacs Lake while State 47 at Anoka goes to the east side.

Either route is a drive through eye-pleasing countryside, with a spectrum of greens from absinthe to zinc. Reached quicker via 169, Mille Lacs Lake is a picturesque eighteen miles long and fourteen miles wide, offering enough game fish to pack every freezer in six states. Rum River State Forest, Kathio State Park, and Ripple River State Wildlife Management Area range along or near the highway, which scoots up the windy west rim of the lake. "Sprucing" up the area around Brainerd are the Pillsbury, Crow Wing, and Wealthwood state forests, which flow in a thick pine-scented flood around that community. Brainerd, an old timber town, prides itself on a history built of wood and water. Several dozen lakes dot the Brainerd backyard. Among them are Gull, Round, North Long, Hubert, Red Sand, Horseshoe, Little Pelican, and Upper Whitefish.

For me, the best route to this semi-wild north country is State 25, which slides through tunnels of spruce and skirts lakes, pools, ponds, sloughs, marshes, and wetlands on its snakelike way to Brainerd. Foley, Jakeville, Silver Corners, Little Rock, Pietz, and other hamlets along the way are separated by miles and miles of forestland, that vast living ocean that sweeps northward to Canada. Some junctions are mere wide spots in the road, where a blink means a miss. At others, you can gas up, grab a candy bar, and smell the sweet balsam perfume emanating from 14.8 million acres of Minnesota woods.

By the time I am thirty minutes beyond the urban roar of the Twin Cities, a settling comes over what was once a frenzied spirit, one harassed by city exhaust, traffic jams, and crabby cab drivers. When this new sense appears, it means "this is the life." Even if the kids spill malted milks over the backseat or Fido has to hit the bushes again, the drive is worth it. The woods start about an hour north of Minneapolis-St. Paul. It's good to stretch and get away from the Twin Cities, whose remaining open spaces are alternately being ogled or gobbled by developers.

To put the history of the region into perspective, be ready to stop at the Mille Lacs Indian Museum, located on the west side of the lake at Indian Point. The current structure, just off US 169, was closed in 1992, and a new $6 million building opens in September 1995. The displays will again depict the lifestyles of several Minnesota tribes whose heritage was shaped by the earth and water. The tiny stucco Little Flower Mission church is across the highway, its rounded roof not quite churchlike but a landmark for years.

A public boat launch at Sha Bosh Kung Bay is north on 169, about two miles from the mission and museum. A five-minute off-road drive from the main road there takes you out to Sha Bosh Kung Point for a scenic picnic spot. Stand on the tip of the rocks, where the breeze is so wonderfully fresh it can almost be seen.

A good day's sightseeing drive is around Mille Lacs Lake on what was old US 169, renamed Lake Frontage Road. A spiderweb of graveled Mille Lacs, Crow Wing, or Aiken county roads from there will also provide an insight into what life is like in north central Minnesota's backcountry. With a day's notice, most resorts in the area can prepare box-style lunches.

Charter fishing on Mille Lacs Lake is a good idea, if you feel a guide would help you find a panfish in the 133,000-acre lake (Minnesota's second largest). Many guides use traditional-style boats, built with low sloping hulls and an open bow that allows lots of room for casting. Since muskie is the fish of choice on Mille Lacs, it is important to have that boat space for flicking out lines. According to old-timers, it takes upwards of 1,000 casts to land a keeper-muskie. The Blue Goose Inn at Garrison on Highway 169 has walls crowded with faded photos of old-time Mille Lacs Lake fishermen and their catches. Everyone is smugly smiling from behind their Bunyan-size mustaches and beards.

To be just as fish happy, you almost need a guide. Almost every store in the area has a bulletin board with listings of qualified anglers who say they know all the lake's secrets. In

Fishing has been the tourism mainstay for generations

addition, tourism publications put out by regional promotion associations often list qualified guides, as well. You can always ask for referrals at any of the numerous bait shops. Resort owners are also helpful.

While fishing has been the tourism mainstay for generations, golfers have discovered the region with a vengeance. Minnesotans are serious about their "woods" and their golfing greens. In fact, twenty-seven public courses are within a thirty-mile radius of Brainerd, helping disperse any too-far-in-the-backwoods feel. Even if you have never hit a golf ball in anger, you can still tell that a property has class, whether from a mere drive-by or a scouting mission along the driveway. A tidy entrance, a profusion of flowers, and an unsolicited hello from a passing staffer have an immediate high-comfort warming effect, at least with me.

Among the many top-rated resorts in the area that present that feel is Izaty's Golf & Yacht Club, host of the 1992, 1993, and 1994 Minnesota PGA championships. Locals say that the 500-acre facility on the south end of Mille Lacs Lake is on the site of an ancient Indian encampment. In fact, the word *izaty* is Dakota for "knife man." The original Camp Izaty was opened in the 1920s by the parents of Dorothy Dubbs. When her folks retired in the 1940s, Dorothy and her husband, Jerry, improved the property by adding a nine-hole golf course. When they were ready to step down in the late 1980s, Minneapolis developer Chip Glaser bought the resort. He subsequently constructed Minnesota's only Dye Designs golf course and added a 120-boat slip on the lake, officially making Izaty's a true golf-and-yacht club. A glass and timbered twenty-eight-room hotel unit was unveiled in 1993, as an add-on for several ranks of existing townhouses. What would Paul Bunyan think?

Located three miles east of US 169 on State 27, Izaty's is forty-five miles south of Brainerd, near the village of Onamia. From Minneapolis—with golf clubs in the trunk—take I-494 or I-694 to I-94 West. At Rogers, pick up State 101 north to Elk River and US 169. Continue north on 169 to State 27 East. Turn right and Izaty's pops out of the forest. The resort's 6,481-yard, eighteen-hole course opened during the 1988 season, offering forty acres of shaggy rough in which to lose a stock of golf balls and forty more acres of water hazards in which to abandon still other balls. Holes 11 and 16 are rated by the state's pros as being two of the snarliest in the state.

The resort is a member of the Audubon Society. The abundant birdhouses scattered around the hedgerows and on the tree limbs are there for a reason: to control insects by non-chemical means. The wrens, robins, and sparrows flit about earning their keep by munching on Minnesota's notorious and much-heralded bug population. In the autumn, three to four eagles usually roost in trees near the lake, making last-minute fishing forays before migrating.

Greenskeeper Steve Schumacher makes sure the birds stay around. He has planted wildflowers in every conceivable spot as a lure, with blue and purple vegetation quilting the grounds in the summer and painting them gold in the autumn. To check out the scope of wildlife, pump around the resort grounds on a bike built for two ($10 for four hours).

Other quality courses in the Mille Lacs Lake-Brainerd range include Breezy Point Resort, Birch Bay, Ruttgers, Whitefish Golf Club, Madder's on Gull Lake, Grand View Lodge, and Mille Lacs Lake Golf Resort. Most are properties that started operating several generations ago and are often in the same family. For instance, Ruttgers first opened in 1898 when a downstate fisherman hopped off the train at Deerwood and asked Grandma Ruttgers if she would cook whatever fish he brought back. She agreed. As more and more fisherfolk showed up at her door (the word got around fast that she was one powerful person at a stove), she went into business.

Always enterprising, Grandpa Ruttgers sensed that diversification would be beneficial. So he fenced off part of a cow pasture for golf. Today, the resort can accommodate 400 guests, some of whom still love fishing while others prefer golf. Staying true to Grandpa's acumen, the facility offers a championship eighteen-hole course for those guests who don't care to fish. Ruttgers, by the way, was selected as one of America's thirty favorite family vacation resorts by *Better Homes & Gardens* in 1993.

Breezy Point near Brainerd was once a haven for gangsters (supposedly complete with slot machines and an escape tunnel in the basement). A Hollywood clientele included honeymooning Clark Gable and Carole Lombard. A house on the grounds where the lovebirds stayed can sleep thirty-four real-people guests today.

For a more extensive listing of golf facilities, the Minnesota Golf Association has a free directory that breaks out the courses by geographical areas around the state. Contact the organization at 6550 York Avenue South, Edina, MN 55435-2335.

Brainerd claims it is the hub city of the state's multi-lake tourism scene. Who can argue? There are some 464 lakes within a thirty-mile radius of the town. Ever since the late nineteenth century, once the logging companies had completed their messy business in the neighborhood, vacationers have appreciated the cool breeze across the rolling waters. This provides a natural air-conditioning on days when faraway city asphalt turns to soup. The first fishing shacks have become multi-activity getaways, with lounges, game rooms, and rentable aqua-skis. But the Brainerd Lakes remain generally pure at their core, even if the country roads are now mostly paved and link resorts rather than small farms. The lodges usually blend into the trees, and deer graze on the golf courses just before the awakening sun crawls over the fluttering white birch. The herds return at dusk, displacing foursomes of duffers with the impunity of animals that still consider this their land.

Simply put, Mille Lacs Lake-Brainerd has stayed a toe-dipping place, whether in the refreshing waters of White Sand, the upper and lower Whitefish cousins, or any of the other lakes. If it rains, and yes, it does, cabin games, songs, and novels easily fill the time. And there is even the potential for family members to communicate meaningfully with each other again.

Typifying the self-reliant type of folks who live in the North Woods, Harold Rademacher, a retired marine welder from Brainerd, built the sixty-passenger *Clamshell Queen* in his backyard when he was in his mid-sixties. He says the project took a year to complete. His wife, Helen, says it took two. Regardless of the real time it took, Rademacher plunged into the task as if he were Noah assembling the Ark. He built the seventy-five-foot-long, twenty-foot-wide paddle wheeler not just for something to do after his retirement, but also to provide an entertainment outlet for handicapped and under-privileged folks. "They didn't have as many chances to get out on the lakes, so I figured this is one way I could help them. We call the *Clamshell Queen* the 'love boat,' where 'love' is not meant in the television sense," he explains. Subsequently, many of his charters are for nursing homes and facilities for the handicapped, in addition to the summer tourist crowd.

Rademacher's dock is directly across the road from Whitefish Golf Club along County 17, thirty miles north of downtown Brainerd and seven miles east of the village of Pequot Lake. That town has a water tower painted red and white to look like a fishing bobber.

Rademacher can cruise on ten of the area's fourteen major interconnected lakes. Although the vessel generally serves charters, drop-by visitors can get on board for $6 if there is space available. Departure times for the 2- to 2.5-hour cruises vary, so check in advance. Wednesday dinner jaunts cast off at 6:00 P.M. There's nothing like kicking back on an early August evening, sitting on the *Clamshell Queen's* upper deck, and knowing that the crew from Rick Beyers' A Pine Restaurant is laying out a steak dinner down below. Beyers is one of the more regular caterers who uses the vessel for dinner parties. The cost for his cruise-and-dinner package is a reasonable $45 for two persons. Call 218-568-8353 for reservations.

Passengers ask a lot of questions, says Rademacher. Samples: How deep are the lakes? Up to 130 feet on the Lower Whitefish and Trout lakes, with an average of thirty to eighty feet elsewhere. Any sharks? No.

Keeping the *Clamshell Queen* a family venture, wife Helen acts as deckhand. Grandson Nick Buffetta earned his captain's license as well as his driver's license when he turned sixteen in 1994. Young Nick had learned the ropes as a deckhand for several years. A brother-in-law, Henry Liners, also captains when Rademacher needs a day off.

Brainerd is now also known for more than just boats, fish, and resorts. The town was placed on the road-racing map several years ago by film star Paul Newman, who popularized the city's tough International Raceway. The course has more curves than the *Sports Illustrated* swimsuit edition and is considered one of the meanest on the pro Formula racing circuit. Newman occasionally drops by to talk cars with contestants and has shaken hands with passersby on Brainerd's principal streets. The main track is not seen from the highway because you must drive down a winding entrance road to the parking area. A campground is attached to the site.

The track is a ten-minute jaunt seven miles from downtown Brainerd by taking State 210 west to State 371 north. The raceway is on the east side of 371, easily spotted because of the huge raceway sign out front. Events begin in early May with rip-roaring Central Road Racing Association motorcycle races and end in September with more motorcycle competition. In between are the cars. The biggest race is usually held the third weekend in August, when the NHRA Champion Auto Stores National attracts from 70,000 to 90,000 people to cheer on their favorite dragsters, stocks, pro stocks, and funny cars—none of which is appropriate for country-road driving. Part of the fun is watching the crowd.

At the race, drivers from around the country compete for more than $900,000 in purses. Since the entire county has only 44,000 residents, the race almost doubles the population. Every hotel, motel, guest house, and stable between Brainerd and St. Cloud fills up, with tourist-info staffers warning race fans to get in their reservations early, early, early.

After the races, many drivers hang out at the Butcher Block restaurant and bar at 1523 Squaw Point Road, northwest of Brainerd on Gull Lake. To get to this hot spot where the talk concentrates on straightaways, fuel mixes, and tires, take State 371 north. Turn west on Gull Dam Road and proceed about five miles. Look for signs pointing the way to the cozy hideaway, with its large windows overlooking the lake. A monster open grill in one of the main dining rooms seems large enough to roast an ox. But a cluster of diners can comfortably stand around the coals and cook individualized steaks. A passel of potatoes are stacked at one end of the grill, to complete the most basic North Woods gourmet meal.

After all the golfing, auto racing, lake cruising, and fishing, the Country Roads wish can still be fulfilled. For a magnificent day's driving, especially in the season of autumn color, a thirty-eight-mile swing begins on County 77, also known as Pine Beach Road, around Gull Lake. To reach 77 from Brainerd, go north five miles to the intersection of State 210 and 371 north. Along the way, look for the flocks of great blue herons often seen around the lowlands. Stop for a quick hike in the Pillsbury State Forest. For another soul-quieting ride (leave the kids at the Paul Bunyan Amusement Center), follow 371 north twelve miles to scenic County 127. Turn east and follow the road past Round Lake to County 115. You skirt Gladstone and Little Hubert lakes on the twenty-mile loop that brings you back to 371.

It is worth it.

In the Area

Akeley Civic and Commerce Association: 800-356-3915
   or 218-652-3230

Brainerd Lakes Area Chamber of Commerce: 800-950-1162
   or 800-450-2838 (Minnesota)

Paul Bunyan Center (Brainerd): 218-829-6342

Mille Lacs Area Tourism Association: 800-346-9375

Lumbertown U.S.A. (Brainerd): 218-829-8872

Izaty's Golf & Yacht Club (Onamia): 800-533-1728

Breezy Point Resort (Pelican Lake): 800-328-2284
   or 800-342-3777 (Minnesota)

Ruttgers Bay Lake Lodge (Deerwood): 800-950-7244
   or 800-450-4545 (Minnesota)

Brainerd International Raceway (Brainerd): 218-829-9836

Grand Casino Mille Lacs: 800-626-LUCK

Clamshell Queen excursion boat (Gull Lake): 218-543-4295

Index

Other titles in the Country Roads series:

Country Roads of Connecticut and Rhode Island
Country Roads of Florida
Country Roads of Hawaii
Country Roads of Illinois, second edition
Country Roads of Indiana
Country Roads of Kentucky
Country Roads of the Maritimes
Country Roads of Massachusetts
Country Roads of Michigan, second edition
Country Roads of New Jersey
Country Roads of New Hampshire
Country Roads of New York
Country Days in New York City
Country Roads of North Carolina
Country Roads of Ohio
Country Roads of Ontario
Country Roads of Oregon
Country Roads of Pennsylvania
Country Roads of Tennessee
Country Roads of Vermont
Country Roads of Virginia
Country Roads of Washington

All books are $9.95 at bookstores.
Or order directly from the publisher (add $3.00
shipping & handling for direct orders):
Country Roads Press
P.O. Box 286
Castine, Maine 04421
Toll-free phone number: **800-729-9179**